Let your lessons become your blessings

Every lesson we endure may not be the best,

but we are blessed.

By Tina M Levene

Let Your Lessons Become Your Blessings
Published by Total Fusion Ministries Press
6475 Cherry Run Rd. Strasburg, OH 44680
www.totalfusionministriespress.org

Copyright © 2013 by Tina M Levene

All rights reserved. No part of this book may be reproduced or transmitted in any form or by any means, electronic or mechanical, including photocopying and recording, or by any information storage and retrieval system, without permission in writing from the publisher.

ISBN - 10:0988370034
ISBN - 13:978-0-9883700-3-6

Cover Design by Michelle Mospens.
Photography by Eric Battershell.

Published in Association with Total Fusion Ministries, Strasburg, OH.

www.totalfusionminsitries.org

I give all appreciation to my Lord, Jesus Christ and my family.

Thank You to Rob Coburn at www.totalfusionministries.org for encouraging me to write this book and Valerie Nielsen for being an incredible editor.

Eric Battershell at www.ericbattershellphotography.com for the beautiful front cover photo.

Michelle Mospens at www.mypersonalartist.com for your graphic design expertise of creating this awesome front and back cover.

This book is dedicated in loving memory to those who went before me: Dawn Marie, Diane, and Chris. May your spirits be renewed in the greatness of our Lord. I miss you and will remember you forever.

I would like to dedicate this book to my family, my 'bestie'-Margaret and all the prayer warriors standing firm beside me throughout my life.

Foreword

*F*rom a small age, we have all learned lessons. Some lessons caused tears, heartache and anger. Other lessons caused joyous screams, jumping up and down, and happiness. Lessons learned from life situations, the good, the bad, and the ugly. This book was written by Tina M Levene to give hope to the hopeless, love to the unloving, and peace to the broken hearted.
This God guided book is an extreme restoration from the depths of darkness and back. It is an affirmation of God's transformation for you from the inside out.

An auto-biography turned devotional, captures the demise of an innocent child by trampling through a treacherous battle of self-indulgence, self-sabotage and restoration back to faith.

Tina's journey will captivate all audiences, young and old, faithful and faithless by teaching a life of surrendering to God, praising God for everything; painful yet promising.

Throughout these teachings you will learn:

- How to prevent someone from stealing your spirit.
- How to control your negative thoughts and words.
- How to speak happiness into your existence.
- How to restore your confidence, faith, love and joy even if you have been challenged by abuse, addiction, atheism, infertility, rape, and physical ailments.
- How to lift up yourself and those around you on a daily basis.

Background

*I*n this book, **Let Your Lessons Become Your Blessings,** you will learn of my lessons, the ones that caused the tears, heartache and anger, and how God has transformed all the anger, hurt and heartache into strength, courage and the desire to help others through their lessons. My journey is nothing less than a miracle, from atheism, being raped, abused, shot at, a knife held to my throat, addicted to drugs, being infertile, losing a baby, breaking my back and many other life lessons that God used to restore my faith.

His gifts of forgiveness, trust and love helped me turn all those lessons into blessings.
My prayer for each of you is that you recognize every lesson you face may not be the best, but you are blessed. Maybe you met a faithful friend during your lesson? God took you to a location you never dreamed of going? God revealed a new job or opportunity for you because of this lesson?

Disclaimer: In no way am I saying I am an expert, medical doctor, or psychologist. This is merely my perception of the challenges I have gone through and the successful story of my life today. Take what you like and leave the rest. By no means am I stating I am perfect, better than or being judgmental of others. I am just stating the facts of my situations, prayerfully, to provide hope and healing to those in need.

I do not use names in this book. If you feel you are part of this journey, please remember these are my perceptions and your perceptions of the same events may be different.

It is not my intention to point the finger at anyone to place blame. What has happened during my journey is over and done with. I have learned from all the situations, and have healed. Please join me on this God given, guided journey to learn how to become a victor instead of a victim.

> *"For I know the plans I have for you, says the Lord. They are plans for good and not for disaster, to give you a future and a hope."* Jeremiah 29:11 (NLT)

Back in the day

*A*s a child, I relished imaginary play. It was safe, fun and I had all the control in the world of who I was, what I was going to say and what I would do. Through playing with my older sister and using our creativity every day, I created a safe place to go to in my head. This place consisted of a warm, soft, comfortable, peaceful haven, a place I like to think of as how heaven may feel, a place I felt safe and true to myself.

I grew up in a home with a strong, alcoholic father, a beautiful, loving mother, and an artistic, hardworking sister (four years older than myself). Today, I can thank God for who He blessed me with as parents and my sibling. My parents did the best with what they had. My sister was my crutch; I leaned on her for everything. She became my go-to person anytime I had an issue or problem. My family tried to protect me from being hurt and they gave me so much.

My mother is the most loving, caring individual I have ever met. She is still my angel on Earth and I am so grateful for her presence in my life. My father is the hardest working person I know.

He has worked for the same company for 47 years and is very loyal to his commitments. His love language is quality time. He is a perfectionist and I am very much like him in that way. Today, I realize I don't have to be the best; I just have to feel blessed.

My mother and father always supported me in extra-curricular activities and sports throughout school. I do not blame them for anything that has happened in my past. They did the best they knew how with what I gave them.

> *"I knew you before I formed you in your mother's womb. Before you were born I set you apart and appointed you as my spokesman to the world."*
> Jeremiah 1:5 (NLT)

I am forever grateful for both of my parents and the love they learned to show me over the years. Who are you grateful for today?

Don't mess up my hair please

*M*y grandparents took us to church once in a while during my childhood and what a joy that was to me. I remember dressing up, which was odd for this tom boy. I felt as if I was a princess getting ready for the ball. Every time we would spend the night at my grandparents' house, she would play Christian music. It was both soothing and peaceful to me.

My grandparents were Christians and loved the church. They took us often, I remember playing in Sunday school, the adults really cared about me and everyone was so happy. I reveled in the fact that they paid attention to me. Even though I enjoyed my time going to church now and then, I did not understand Jesus or what being a Christian meant.

My family stopped attending church for a while. Then we started attending another church near our house. I was baptized at a Methodist Church when I was 13 years old. The only thing I could think of during the ceremony was that the Reverend was messing up my nicely feathered hair. It was the 80's, people! I remember getting a certificate, but the obsession of my wet head overwhelmed me more than the appreciation of the baptism.

> *"From the time he was baptized by John until the day he was taken from us into heaven. Whoever is chosen will join us as a witness of Jesus' resurrection."* Acts 1:22 (NLT)

What does it mean to you to be baptized?

Appreciate the time you have now

At the age of seven, my friend was kidnapped, raped, and murdered. This was a turning point in my life. I believed no one was to be trusted, nothing was safe and my life should have ended tragically, too. I remember the hurt of not seeing my friend ever again, not playing with her and not seeing her smiling eyes or listening to her laughter.

Law enforcement officers searched for what felt like years for her missing body. I remember searching in the woods for her body or clues. I just wanted to find something. I wanted to find a clue to where she had gone, who had taken her and why I could not have stopped them. Her murderer admitted to killing her and took the police to recover her battered body left in a field.

As I am writing this, tears are flowing down my cheeks as if this all happened yesterday. The emotions are still raw and the void of her absence is still there. Questions often rush throughout my head each day: what would she look like today? Where would she have worked? Would she have children of her own? Would we still be friends?

Her funeral was a closed casket due to the wrecked mash her murderer left behind; I remember the long lines to greet her family. The minutes it took to move to the front of the line felt like hours. I do not remember any adult ever counseling me, telling me it was not my fault or that it was not okay what that sick man did to her helpless, tiny body.

From this point forward in my life, I did not feel safe, secure or appreciated inside my body or outside. I had survivor's guilt. I would ask myself questions like, *Why didn't I stop this from happening? How come I am still alive and she's dead?* Questions a seven year old surely should not be asking themselves on a daily basis.

> *"The Lord is close to the brokenhearted; he rescues those who are crushed in spirit."* Psalm 34:18 (NLT)

Who have you lost in your childhood? What do you miss about them?

I'll show you, I'll hurt me!

At the age of nine, I picked up a cigarette butt off the ground and smoked it. I coughed and coughed but the power of the nicotine rushed through my brain. I was hooked. I stole cigarettes as often as possible to smoke. The risk of being caught gave me a sudden high; the deep inhale of the smoke filling my mouth immediately released all the anger and frustration I held in my heart. This was the beginning of an addict's love affair with a drug. The defiance, power of choosing what I do to my body and my brain empowered me as a young smoker.

At the age of 14, I found a bottle of wine in my refrigerator, which was odd since my father quit drinking alcohol when I was four years old. It was my mother's alcohol and she was one of those social drinkers, so the bottle was probably a year old and quite full.

My friend and I decided to share it. She had a few drinks and was disgusted by the taste. I, on the other hand, was not drinking it for the taste; it was for pure motivation of indulgence, affect, and defiance. I drank the rest of the bottle and from there on out, my drinking career began.

> *"Be careful! Watch out for attacks from the Devil, your great enemy. He prowls around like a roaring lion, looking for some victim to devour."* 1 Peter 5:8 (NLT)

How have your friends influenced you and the decisions you have made?

How do you feel comfortable in an uncomfortable life?

*A*s a teenager, I was raped by an individual I trusted and knew for many years. He controlled what I wore, what I would say, how I would feel and who I would talk to. This was supposed to be a person I trusted, felt comfortable with and thought had my best interests at heart.

Instead, he became a ruler, a dictator and an abuser that controlled my every emotion. If he was angry at someone or something, I had no choice but to adopt that same emotion: anger. This was a very abusive relationship. I received physical, emotional and psychological trauma from him, someone who told me he loved me. I endured the abuse for one year; one minute too many but just enough time to distort my perception of relationships for the rest of my life. His abuse distorted the shape of all my relationships for a long time.

Quickly after this and many disheartening relationships, I began dating another young man who held a gun to my forehead, pulled the trigger and laughed hysterically as I reacted in fear. I remember him laughing and sarcastically saying, It's not like it's loaded! He tilted the gun in front of his chest, glanced down at the gun and found one bullet in the chamber. It was in the very next chamber to be executed if he pulled the trigger again. One more pull of the trigger and I would have been shot in the forehead. I would have died before the age of 20.

> *"For he orders his angels to protect you wherever you go."*
> Psalm 91:11 (NLT)

How has God saved your life from a harmful past?

Never give up who you are, to be with someone you are not

My rampage of destructive relationships led to no self-esteem, no self-respect and no control. I remember thinking I had to have a relationship with a male or I was not worthy. If a man did not value me and my body, I was depressed, sad, and suicidal. My relationships broke my heart repeatedly because I would give my partner everything: my heart, my mind and my respect. And what did I get in return? I got cheated on, disrespected and taken advantage of.

Today, I realize love doesn't hurt. No one should emotionally, physically or psychologically damage me. But more importantly, I will not allow that to happen ever again in my life. No person is worth my time or energy if the consequence will lead to the ruin of my soul or spirit.

> *"When you go through deep waters and great trouble, I will be with you. When you go through rivers of difficulty, you*

will not drown! When you walk through the fire of oppression, you will not be burned up; the flames will not consume you."
Isaiah 43:2-3 (NLT)

How do you respect your body today? Who do you trust?

To find out who you are, you must know who you were

*A*t the beginning of my college years, I had no self-esteem, no desire to live and my drinking began to control me. So what does a young person do? I began using drugs to escape the hurt, despair and heartlessness of bonding with another human being. It was a fear driven battle to wake up each day.

Marijuana fulfilled my search for peace, calmness and pleasure. I could sit and marvel in my creativity as if I were a child again. The illusion was that no one could hurt me when I was high on weed. At least, my brain was not acknowledging the fear of being hurt. However, the paranoia grew more and more every day until a day I thought I was having a heart attack. My dependency on marijuana began as a way to prevent panic attacks on a daily basis and to relax to feel normal since I was naturally hyperactive.

A game of running from self awareness, life and the challenges within me continued along with destructive relationships. I remember standing in front of a mirror with a razor to my wrist, crying uncontrollably and thinking… if only… if only I had that perfect boyfriend, if only I was beautiful, if only I had not allowed my friend to be murdered!

These cries were deafening compared to the loneliness that haunted me every day. The darkness dwelled throughout my head and heart. I started building a brick wall around me so no one could hurt me again.

By this time, I was using alcohol and drugs daily, flunking out of college and the only prayers I would undeservingly throw up to Him were pleas to save my pitiful life after a night of partying. Please God don't let me die! Please God get me out of this mess!

> *"That is why I tell you, don't worry about everyday life- whether you have enough food and drink, enough clothes to wear. Isn't life more than food, and your body more than clothing?"* Matthew 6: 25 (NLT)

Do you believe that God will provide all your needs for you today?

Who are you running from?

*M*y battle of fighting, stealing, running from the police and lying was the adrenalin seeking roller coaster ride I hung onto for years. During the college classes I did attend, I was high or drunk. If it was not for my roommate taking notes and helping me study, I would have failed. She provided me with rides, money and food. I will forever be grateful to her and many of my other college friends and roommates that helped me.

By this time, my parents told me they were not paying for a party and cut me off financially. This challenging decision they made saved my life. For an addict, having enablers in your life is like putting rose colored sun glasses on. Everything appears to be cool until those enablers rip the glasses off your face and crush them to reveal to you a clear vision of your unmanageable life.

I had a path of reckless relationships, multiple pregnancy scares, overdoses, and ER visits. I was stealing, had been shot at, had a knife held to my throat, was raped, used drugs I said I never would, barely escaped many violent and criminal acts, but worst of all ... I could not look at myself in the mirror. I had no dignity, no respect and no desire to live. Who was I really running from? Myself!

> *"Honor your father and mother. Then you will live a long, full life in the land the LORD your God is giving you."* Exodus 20:12 (NLT)

Are you running from something? Why?

Keep your face to the sunshine and you cannot see the shadows.
~ Helen Keller

After a night of horror – no really, it was Halloween! – I attended yet another party and was so high I didn't remember much. The next day, my friends shared with me that I was acting so rude that in the middle of conversations, I would walk away from them while they were still speaking to me. This, for me, was one of those lines I created in my head – the line of, if I hurt anyone else like I had been hurt, I would quit whatever it was I was doing.

This was conveniently at a time in my college days when the university I was attending sent me a letter stating I was being dismissed for failure to attend classes and for academic failure. This led me, while drunk, to handwrite a plea for mercy to the university for my college career to continue. I said in the letter that I had a drug problem with marijuana and I had stopped. I promised I would focus on my courses and that I would not ruin this opportunity. They accepted me back on academic probation.

> *"So let us come boldly to the throne of our gracious God. There we will receive his mercy, and we will find grace to help us when we need it."* Hebrews 4:16 (NLT)

How has God showed you mercy in your life?

What is my purpose? Do I even have one?

On a wintery day after many nights on my knees pleading to whomever was up there to save me from yet another self-inflicted night of horrific acts, I finally attended a class. The professor was a beautiful Christian woman. I completed the presentation I wrote about <u>How children deal with the death of other children</u>.

During my presentation, I cried, I was angry, I was heartbroken and the class cried with me. Though the paper was written using researched facts about grieving, I had not dealt with my own grief until I read it out loud and saw the reactions of my classmates.

The professor kept me after class and asked what I was majoring in. I told her it was Interior Design. She quickly instructed me to change it to Family & Child Development. She proceeded to share with me that my purpose was to help children. I did not even like kids at that time! I replied back, *What? Are you kidding me? This is my second year in college and you want me to change my degree?* But I did because this was the one person in my life who believed in me. She gave me a purpose to wake up to every day.

> *"Look at my Servant, whom I have chosen. He is my Beloved, and I am very pleased with him, and he will proclaim justice to the nations. He will not fight or shout; he will not raise his voice in public. He will not crush those who are weak, or quench the smallest hope, until he brings full justice with his final victory. And his name will be the hope of all the world."*
> Matthew 12: 18-21 (NLT)

What is your purpose?

Hope

I began dating a counselor; it was very convenient to have free counseling while in a relationship. Till this day, I have no idea what he saw in me. Maybe he wanted to rescue me; maybe he wanted to use me as a field experiment. Whatever his motive, it worked. He changed my life.

I shared my life with him: my friend's murder, growing up in an alcoholic family, being raped and abused and my drug problem with marijuana. Mind you, we were usually drunk when I would share all these experiences. They do not call alcohol 'liquid courage' for nothing.

Nevertheless, this new boyfriend brought light into my life. He helped me see the positive. He was a survivor of cancer and he believed everyday was a gift. I believe now that God knew the only way He could speak to me was through this spiritual individual.

My new boyfriend suggested I go to a 12 step recovery program, a support group for family and friends of alcoholics. I spoke to my sister about it and we agreed we would go together. Little did I know, this would be leading me on a journey of recovery... healing me from the inside out.

> *"Wait patiently for the Lord. Be brave and courageous. Yes, wait patiently for the Lord."*
> Psalm 27:14 (NLT)

Has someone given you hope in your life? Who was it and how did they do it?

Getting the tools for change

I was familiar with a 12 step recovery program because my father used to take me with him when I was young, so I was not very frightened to attend one meeting. One meeting is all I needed to be cured. Right?

I walked through the doors of the old, Catholic Church basement and an older, angelic woman walked towards me. She put her arms out to hug me and welcomed me. I thought to myself, how do I throw this woman on the floor in a wrestling move to hurt her before she will hurt me? Unfortunately, for many years, the only reason someone wanted to hug me was to have sex with me. Intimacy only led to sex at this time in my life. I was afraid to let someone close to me, to even touch me.

> *"But when I am afraid, I put my trust in you."* Psalm 56:3 (NLT)

How have your past hurts affected your ability to bond with people?

Some are sicker than others

During the first 12 step recovery program meeting, I sat with my arms folded in front of me and thought, *These people are so weak they should... They need to... .* I thought I had all the answers for them. I would say to myself, *If they were only as tough as me.* You see, even though I had no self-esteem and felt horrible about my self-image, I felt I had all the answers for everyone else. I thought I knew how people should live their lives. I would say to myself, *If only people listened to me, they wouldn't get hurt!* I had made it my mission to save everyone, but I could not even save myself.

Then one day it hit me, *How has that worked for you, Tina?* It hadn't, so I sought out a sponsor as suggested.

She was calm, peaceful, and gentle; everything I was not. She worked with me on understanding a Higher Power because I did not believe in God, Jesus or anything at this time. I despised Jesus freaks, Bible bashers or those judgmental perfectionists!

My sponsor would explain to me in such a gentle manner that I cannot make a sunrise or sunset. That God did not punish me all those years through rape, abuse and murdering my friend. She was such an inspiration to me.

Every day I would have to call her and list five things I was grateful for that day. I challenge you to do that for six months. Try not to repeat your gratitude list. It will change your attitude towards life forever.

I began to understand that there is a Higher Power and I called him God. I started working the 12 steps of this 12 step recovery program with her.

Step 1: Admitted I was powerless over people, places and things and that my life had become unmanageable. I interpreted this as though I had no control over other people. I cannot control if something goes wrong, breaks or does not go the way I planned. I do have the power over me, my thoughts, my decisions and my reactions. What a relief! I only am responsible for me. To summarize Step 1: I can't!

We moved to **Step 2: Came to believe that a Power greater than ourselves could restore us to sanity.** Okay, at this point I acknowledged there's a 'Big Man upstairs' but now I have to trust that He will do His job? Are you kidding me? Every man in my life was negative, conniving, manipulative, abusive and not trustworthy. As you can tell, I had a VERY difficult time with this step. Needless to say, I had a very hard time trusting anyone, let alone men.

It was suggested I write a list of all the qualities I wanted in a husband. So, I wrote a three page list of qualities from Sense of Humor to Caring. Then I was told, *That is your Higher Power.* I argued! I was gently led back to the first step: my life is unmanageable and it can only get better by letting God help me. To summarize step 2: He can!

Step 3 was a little easier since I figured out the What and Who. Now came the trusting part. **Step 3: Made a decision to turn our will and our lives over to the care of God as we understood Him**. At this point, I understood God as a caring, loving, would-do-anything-for-'ya type of guy. I started to understand that God saved me all those nights I was shot at, when I was in harm's way. God was there for me, when I was not there for Him. To summarize step 3: I am going to let Him!

> *"It is better to trust the Lord than to put confidence in people."* Psalm 118:8 (NLT)

How has your life become unmanageable today?

Starting to feel comfortable in my own skin

During my recovery, I started to feel a heaviness being lifted off my back. I could raise my chin up. I could even look in the mirror without disgust. I learned that no one can make me feel a certain way without my permission to do so. My feelings are my own. And those feelings are not facts. The 3 C's saved my life:

1. I didn't **C**ause it.
2. I can't **C**ontrol it.
3. I can't **C**ure it.

I applied these principles in all aspects of my life. And my life started to change for the better. I learned that when I met someone, I could chose to share with them what has happened in my life or I could keep it to myself. That I am only as sick as my secrets. I do not have to trust everyone or like everyone I meet. My motto is: Principles above personalities. This helps me in my personal life as well as my professional life.

"The Lord is my rock, my fortress, and my savior; my God is my rock, in whom I find protection. He is my shield, the strength of my salvation, and my stronghold." Psalm 18:2 (NLT)

How do your secrets make you sick? Do you have someone in your life you can trust to share your secrets with? Who would that be?

Let go and let God

This 12 step recovery program helped me in all my relationships. I learned positive ways to communicate, to cope and to control myself as well as my actions. So much of my growth was during these first three steps in this 12 step recovery program. I began to realize that when dealing with an addict, I should look at them as if they have their diagnosis, Addict, written across their forehead or treat them like they are dying. To remember their behavior is the result of their disease, not the result of who they truly are. This tool helps to create mercy for them.

One of the best aspects of intrapersonal skill building I learned through this 12 step recovery program was that expectations of others are premeditated resentments. I expected people to act or do for me what they clearly were not capable of doing. Then I would get angry at them because they did not perform to my expectation.

If you want to live a life of constantly being let down by human beings, keep having expectations for them to be perfect. Today, God exceeds all my expectations. His perfection through His son, Jesus saves me every day. Yes, today, I am a Jesus Freak.

> *"Trust in the Lord with all your heart; do not depend on your own understanding. Seek His will in all you do, and he will direct your paths."* Proverbs 3:5 (NLT)

What expectations do you often have of others? How have those expectations let you down?

Take what you like & leave the rest

I learned to listen to others; take what I liked and I left the rest. Also, I tried not to solve their problems. I heard a saying, *Who am I to tell you how you should live your journey?* That is so true. If anyone interfered in my life before recovery, I would just get angry and resentful toward them and boldly escort them out of my life.

They were just another person I would dismiss from my life. I believe my journey brought me to the rooms of a 12 step recovery program to save my life and through saving my life, God is using me as His vessel to save others' lives. Today, it begins and ends with God, not Tina.

If my life went according to my way, I would have definitely sold myself short. I have so many blessings today because of God's perfect planning of His will for me. Not my will, but His.

My relationships started to improve through learning new ways to live a healthy life. I dated a strong, young man that had a few years of sobriety. He taught me so much and I admired his joyous and free attitude. He was cool and sober! But he moved over 1000 miles away and inevitably we had to break up.

One quote I liked was: Pity is feeling sorry, love is never saying sorry. I started to understand that my feelings are my own. I am worthy to have feelings. And no one needs to tell me otherwise.

> *"For I can do everything with the help of Christ who gives me the strength I need."* Philippians 4:13 (NLT)

Who gave you insight to the positive changes you could make in your life? Have you made those changes? If not, what is holding you back?

Walk in the newness of the light of your life

After many months in this 12 step recovery program, I was working the 4th step with my sponsor. This is when the real power of change happened for me. Once I began focusing on what I could control – myself and my choices – I took the attention and energy off of trying to control others. I started becoming aware of my defense mechanisms, my coping skills and how I would project my issues onto others so I would not have to deal with them myself.

I remember sitting on my knees in my college bedroom floor crying because I was trying to control my drinking at this time. I had a calendar I would schedule when I could drink but it seemed there was always a time to drink and my scheduled drinking extravaganzas became unscheduled and uncontrollable.

I had switched from drinking anything with alcohol in it, to wine. Wine is recommended by doctors, it is healthy. Right? Actually, I have learned that it is actually the antioxidants from grapes that are healthy and you can get the same nutritional value from grape juice. But it is a classy drink right? Alcoholics surely do not drink wine do they?

I sat on my bedroom floor feeling sad, depressed and the devil was telling me lies. It said you are worthless, you won't amount to anything and you should be dead. I was worn out, felt powerless and had so much more work to do on myself.

Immediately, my CD player turned on and played a reggae song by Big Mountain, the <u>Upful and Bright</u> song says, *Don't worry, don't you worry, 'cause God's on your side. And you're healthy and bright.*

Till this day, I believe God played that song for me to give me hope. I got up off the floor, dusted myself off and prayed to God for strength and His will to be done in my life.

> ***"God saved you by his special favor when you believed. And you can't take credit for this; it is a gift from God."*** Ephesians 2:8 (NLT)

How has God spoken to you? Have you listened?

If you have to control something, it's already out of control

I was scheduling days to get drunk, trying to control my trustless relationships, struggling with depression and school work as well as jobs. I was going to bars by myself, driving drunk, and doing everything I said I would never do because it would define me as an alcoholic.

As an alcoholic, I would find every excuse to drink alcohol. If I was celebrating a holiday, I would drink. If I was sad, I would drink. If the day ended in the letter 'y', I would drink!

By this time, I was drinking uncontrollably and dating a different drinking buddy. I would find men that drank as much or more than me, even though most of them did not really know how much I drank because I was not one to brag. For me to brag, would be shouting from the mountain tops of the world that I was, in fact, an alcoholic!

On January 30, 1998, my friend and I bought five kegs – lots of liquor – and started drinking alcohol at 4:30 p.m. that day. I remember all the kegs running dry, the liquor was gone and I was not drunk yet. This was 13 hours after our first drink together. My friend was passed out. I woke him up by screaming at him, asking how he could have let all the alcohol run out. I will never forget the look in his eyes; it was of fear, confusion and sadness that after 13 hours of drinking, I was angry that there was no more alcohol left to drink.

I was a functioning drunk. Never vomited, never passed out and always had a fresh, new drink in my hand during that day and night. When everyone else was trashed, I was still walking around functioning. This scared me sober.

> *"Submit to God and you will have peace; then things will go well for you."* Job 22:21 (NLT)

What has happened in your life that scared you? Have you changed it?

To each their own

I finally fell asleep at 5:30am and woke up at 9 a.m. to go to my 12 step recovery program meeting. Even though I knew my blood alcohol level was outrageous, I felt good enough to drive to the meeting. I sat next to my sister and she kept looking at me as if she was concerned about something. After the meeting, she asked me why I smelled so bad. I felt humiliated to admit that I spent the last 13 hours drinking alcohol, got home at 5:30am and literally woke up at 9 a.m. and jumped into my car for that meeting.

After the meeting, a friend from this 12 step recovery program asked me to join her for lunch. This is where God does for us what we cannot do for ourselves. This young lady, the same age as me began sharing her story of alcoholism. It did not sound exactly like mine because she had gotten married early in life, had a baby and worked full-time but her feelings of guilt, shame, frustration and powerlessness were the same as mine.

I walked away from that lunch knowing in my heart, I was an alcoholic. At 23 years old, I had to surrender to the fact that as an alcoholic

I am allergic to alcohol and that my drinking was not normal. The Big Book of a 12 step recovery program explains it all so clearly. God, that book and the Bible saved my life.

The next day, I immediately called a psychologist at the University I attended to get an evaluation for free. When I sat on his couch, I started answering his questions. I heard the source of my frustrations all stemming from my alcohol abuse.

Every time I would complain about a person (boyfriend, family member, friend), the psychologist would ask *Were you drinking alcohol or under the influence of alcohol when that fight occurred?* I started to see the vicious cycle of dysfunction that revolved around my alcohol abuse. I cried and screamed at him, I am just so sick! He replied with a yawn, *You just have a problem with alcohol!*

That was enough confirmation for me to drive down to my parents' house over 30 minutes away. It was a Tuesday night, so I knew my father would be going to his 12 step recovery program home group meeting. I knocked on the door and my surprised father opened it.

I said *Dad, I think I'm a pickle!* My father looked at me a bit puzzled and asked *What's a pickle?* Lord only knows what he thought because this poor man has received various phone calls, and endured stressful circumstances and financial difficulties all because of me and my mishaps. I think he thought I meant I was a lesbian at first, but I quickly replied back to him *Dad, I was a cucumber, but I've had too much juice! Now I'm a pickle!*

Without hesitation, this man that I have witnessed being transformed over the years in this 12 step recovery program, with great concern asked *Does that mean you want to go to my 12 step recovery program meeting with me tonight?*

This was the man that I sat on his lap in his big recliner in the basement at the age of three and became his beer retriever, now we were sitting beside each other at a 12 step recovery program meeting. He loved me back then but was unable to show it because alcohol became the barricade of his destruction. Through the help of his 12 step recovery program, he became the father I never had, someone I am proud to call 'Daddy', and a human being I love as a friend not just as a relative.

I do not think I would ever have 'crossed over to the other side' to this 12 step recovery program from the other 12 step recovery program without my father asking me to attend my first meeting with him. He was supportive, loving and introduced me to all his friends (which consisted of mostly older men and one older woman) which they all loved me no matter what.

My first meeting had a speaker that led the meeting. He spoke about his failed marriages, numerous DUI's, loss of children and friends. Even though I could not relate much to the specifics of his story, I heard all the 'isms' of his disease: the lying, manipulation, conniving, and baffling craziness of alcoholism and how it rips apart people's lives. I could relate to his hopelessness, his battle every day with trusting others and his feelings of inadequacy. I knew I had come home.

I will forever be grateful for my father's forgiveness, unconditional love and willingness to pray for me at times I didn't even believe in God. My parents loved me even when I did not love myself. I had arrived home in the rooms of this 12 step recovery program, a place to feel free, recover and learn how to live life without alcohol.

> *"Stop judging others, and you will not be judged. Stop criticizing others, or it will all come back on you. If you forgive others, you will be forgiven. If you give, you will receive. Your gift will return to you in full measure, pressed down, shaken together to make room for more, and running over. Whatever measure you*

use in giving-large or small-it will be used to measure what is given back to you." Luke 6:37-38 (NLT)

Who has shown you unconditional love in your life? Have you returned it?

It was time to change people, places and things

I was 23 years old, living at college with three of my drinking buddies – two males and one female. Alcohol was everywhere. I had to smell the orange juice before drinking it because I knew what I was putting in it when I drank it, and it was not ice. And I had a job as a waitress delivering alcohol to tables every night. Yet, I remained sober because I clearly knew I was done drinking, period.

I remember learning in the other 12 step recovery program you have to change people, places and things. This to me was my whole environment – who I dated, where I worked, and who I hung around with. I spoke to my roommates, who were wonderful. They did not have a clue that I had struggled with alcoholism. I had always had the gift of deception. They agreed that I could move out a few months before my lease was up. I was so blessed they understood and supported me. My parents invited me to live with them for the time being while I cleaned up my life.

"But the Lord said to Samuel, Don't judge by his appearance or height, for I have rejected him. The Lord doesn't make decisions the way you do! People judge by outward appearance, but the Lord looks at a person's thoughts and intentions." 1 Samuel 16:7 (NLT)

Like autumn leaves and snowflakes, remember that each of us are God's handiwork and we are all different but special. Do you respect God's master piece, which is you to change people, places and things?

It's so hard to say goodbye

I was dating a drinking buddy and I shared with him my new found freedom from alcohol. He was supportive at first, and then I remember him saying a few weeks after I was sober, he missed his party girl. This was a very caring, loving young man; he was definitely the most patient man I dated. We agreed it was time to end the relationship due to my changed priority of sobriety. I was heartbroken as I left his apartment because I did love him, but if he questioned if he could love the new me, then I could not sacrifice what I needed to do in my life for him.

> *"Guard your heart above all else, for it determines the course of your life."* Proverbs 4:23 (NLT)

Who have you had to say good bye to in your life? Was it a healthy decision?

90 meetings in 90 days

When I got sober, January 31, 1998, it was suggested I do 90 meetings in 90 days. I think I did 116 meetings in 90 days on my own. I met the most caring, heartfelt, supportive individuals in the rooms of this 12 step recovery program. I attended speaker meetings but loved discussion meetings. These meetings were based on either a question/answer format or a Big Book discussion study group. I was like a dried out sponge just slurping up everything as if I was a baby just learning to walk on their own. It was amazing how God started transforming me from the inside out.

In the Big Book, it states that it does not matter the age, or how long a person has drank alcohol to qualify as an alcoholic. Early in sobriety, the older men in this program would say to me I spilled more alcoholic drinks then you ever drank young one. I quickly replied with Well, maybe if you would have drunk the alcohol instead of spilling it, you would have found this program at my age too!

"Don't let the excitement of youth cause you to forget your

Creator. Honor him in your youth before you grow old and no longer enjoy living. It will be too late then to remember him, when the light of the sun and moon and stars is dim to your old eyes, and there is no silver lining left among the clouds."
Ecclesiastes 12:1-2 (NLT)

What changes do you need to make in your life today? How will you handle people that are not supportive of your changes?

Searching for peaceful endings within

I had found a sponsor that had experience in both 12 step recovery programs. She guided me through my 5th step: a fearless moral inventory. This step can be scary to so many in recovery, but for me it was a relief! I thought, *I can actually list all the horrible things I have done to others and my sponsor will still love me even knowing the darkness of my soul?*

I listed all my character defects and amends as if you just asked me a simple question. Flabbergasted, my sponsor suggested I list all my positive attributes, too. I was stumped!

I had focused on all my negative, character defects and short comings for so long that for me to switch my thinking to positive attributes was like asking a leopard to change their spots. I did my best to list a few, I started with I am caring.

For some reason, I had abandonment issues. I thought that if I said or did something wrong, people would leave me forever. I soon learned that I can only control myself and my motives.

If someone does not want to be part of my life, that is their decision, not mine.

I learned to not be a people pleaser anymore and not put my energy into manipulating others. An old timer told me, take all the energy you would put into trying to change, manipulate, steal, cheat, and lie to others and put that time and energy into your sobriety. I did and I spent a lot of time reading the Big Book, attending meetings and working the 12 steps with my sponsor. I am so grateful for program and their members.

> *"But those who wait on the Lord will find new strength. They will fly high on wings like eagles. They will run and not grow weary. They will walk and not faint."* Isaiah 40:31 (NLT)

How have you tried controlling others in your life? How has that hurt your relationship?

No relationships for the first year of sobriety

Okay, so some guidance that was recommended in this new program of recovery, I did not follow. It was suggested that you do not have a relationship in the first year of sobriety. Instead, I met a sober man on the internet. We met up in a different state, and after months of dating, we got engaged and started living together, all within my first year of sobriety.

I do NOT recommend anyone doing this. Within my first year and a half of sobriety, my fiancé cheated on me, became very emotionally abusive and relapsed, and my sponsor relapsed and was missing. I was so grateful for the understanding I had learned in the other 12 step recovery program, to focus on what I need to do to live a healthy, functioning life.

I moved out of my fiancé's apartment, thanks to my Dad. I got a new loving sponsor and continued my sobriety. I only have control over myself and have to focus on 'cleaning up the crap in my yard'. I have no right looking over the fence into someone else's yard and judging them for the choices they have made, when my yard is a mess!

> *"Stop judging others, and you will not be judged. For others will treat you as you treat them. Whatever measure you use in judging, it will be used to measure how you be judged. Why worry about a speck in your friend's eye when you have a log in your own? How can you think of saying, 'Let me help you get rid of that speck in your eye, when you can't see past the log in your own eye? Hypocrite! First get rid of the log from your own eye; then perhaps you will see well enough to deal with the speck in your friend's eye."* Matthew 7:1-5 (NLT)

What can you do so others' unhealthy decisions do not affect your life?

Lost but not forgotten

As you can imagine, as so many of us do, I have a really hard time with death. Unfortunately, I have had to attend a lot of my friends and family members' funerals.

I remember attending a 12 step recovery program meeting and meeting this woman who had a smile that just made you smile, too. A laugh that made me laugh. She was patient, so sweet and a great friend. I spent one weekend with her camping. She was such a down to earth type of woman, loved boating, fishing and just talking. She was one of those friends that you could talk and talk to, then look at the clock and eight hours flew by.

This woman committed suicide and till this day, I have no idea why. She was happy, unselfish, loving and learning a new way of life that enabled her to better her marriage, family relationships and friendships.

I remember driving down the highway after finding out she killed herself. I was so angry. I was screaming up at the sky, pounding on the steering wheel, yelling out questions hoping to get some answers.

Then, of course, the survivor guilt kicked in: *Why did I not save her? How could I let this happen?* The CD played over and over again in my head as if it was skipping back to the age of seven, when my friend was murdered. I immediately knew I had to pray about her, her family and the acceptance of this. I did not like that it happened, but I had to accept that it happened. I felt hurt and angry. I spoke to other friends, I spoke to my sponsor and most importantly, I forgave her.

> *"God saved you by his grace when you believed. And you can't take credit for this; it is a gift from God."* Ephesians 2:8 (NLT)

How has someone's suicide affected your life? Are you still angry?

God will take care of me

*A*fter college graduation, I was hired at the agency where I completed my internship. I still have no idea why they risked all they did to employ me there. I had a few months of sobriety and they loved and supported me as if I was their own child. It was an incredible agency; my supervisors were great and my co-workers, caring and thoughtful.

I was a case manager for children at this mental health agency. I had a case load of 32 rambunctious children ages 2-17. I lived by myself with my dog; I worked at this job for over 50 hours a week for a measly $18,000 a year income. It was one of the happiest times of my life.

I truly loved the children I worked with each day. It was challenging some days being called obscenities, being hit or having feces thrown at me, but nothing could stop me from caring about them. They were merely innocent victims born to the dysfunction their parents created. I never placed blame on them or felt negatively about them.

God is so good all the time. He gave me this job because each one of my clients had a bit of my story in them. One lost their friend to murder, one was raped, one was abused, one was raised in an alcoholic family, one struggled with her own addictions. It was as if God said, *"Tina, I brought you through all these lessons so you can help these children see the light, which is me, God."*

After over two years of working in this intense, challenging job, I found a job that paid more money and was less stressful. I asked myself, *But what will my clients do without me?* I prayed for God to protect each of them and I visualized putting them all in my hand and giving them to God.

Goodbyes were extremely hard with these little ones. A nine year old girl cried and cried as I told her that I enjoyed spending time with her as her case manager and I tried to give her hope for the future. She walked me to my car and as I was driving away after my last day of work, she waved me down to stop me. I abruptly stopped my car, rolled down my window as she walked to my window crying again. She said, *"Don't worry about me Ms. Tina, God will take care of me!"* And with what she said she gestured up to heaven by pointing with her finger. I drove off feeling confident that she was left in the best hands, God's hands.

"Let us see your miracles again; let our children see your glory at work." Psalm 90:16

Have you had to let go of someone in your life? Do you feel that God will take care of them?

Progress rather than perfection

As if I had not learned my lesson already, I jumped into yet another dysfunctional relationship with another sober man I met on the internet and moved in with him. The move was initiated because I had to file charges on a child I worked with since he came to school with a gun to kill me.

I had to resign from the job I loved and move out of the apartment I lived in alone. This man was a recovered alcoholic, sober, and a successful business man. He employed me, housed me and fed me. He had a daughter he had custody of and even though I loved children, it was hard on her to have me pop into her life, live in her home and play mom.

I learned a lot from that relationship. One day, we went sled riding on a huge hill in Cleveland at a state park. At the top of the hill, I told my boyfriend's daughter and pregnant sister that I wanted to go down the hill first to make sure it was safe for them. I am so glad I did. While flying down this snowy hill at top speeds, I did not realize there was a three foot snowboarding ramp made out of icy snow at the bottom. I flew up about six feet high and landed on my head. My boyfriend immediately called 911. I was rushed to the Emergency Room in the ambulance and every examination was performed to identify any broken bones in my back and neck.

The doctor was amazed that I did not break my neck or back. He said because of all the years in gymnastics and being athletic, I had built up muscles in my neck and shoulders that saved my life. All my life I was embarrassed when people asked me why I had such broad, muscular shoulders. That day I thanked God for building me that way. I spent many days in bed, trying to recover.

I lived in the upstairs apartment of this man's house. I remember lying in bed in pain; my dog had scratched my nose making it bleed because he was licking the tears off my cheeks and pressing his paws upon them. There I was laying in a bed, in this man's house, nose bleeding, crying, hungry, had urinated the bed, in pain and the man was nowhere to be found. It was that moment I realized I had isolated myself from the people that truly cared about me over a relationship with a man I really did not know and who was preoccupied with his own life.

I called my sister and she offered to take me in with her and her family. I got into my car wearing only my slippers and pajamas, driving through a blizzard with just my left hand due to the injuries to my neck and right shoulder, crying the whole hour and a half drive to my sister's house. When I arrived, I was so grateful to be alive and that she would take care of me. Between my parents and her, I was nursed back to health. It was that moment I realized, *I am single, I have no children and I should travel and see the world!* So, I applied for work on a cruise ship.

> *"Why be like the pagans who are so deeply concerned about these things? Your heavenly Father already knows all your needs, and He will give you all you need from day to day if you live for Him and make the Kingdom of God your primary concern. So don't worry about tomorrow, for tomorrow will bring its own worries. Today's trouble is enough for today."*
> Matthew 6: 32-34 (NLT)

Yesterday is history, tomorrow is a mystery, today is a gift; that's why it's called the present. Are you grateful for your life today? Why?

Everything happens for a reason

I flew from Akron to Miami to start my first day of training to work on a cruise ship. Then I worked two weeks on a ship. After that contract, I was flown home and quickly began applying to other cruise lines. I loved working on this floating city!

Some people in this 12 step recovery program criticized my decision to work on a cruise ship. In the Big Book of this 12 step recovery program, it states that the alcoholic is like a man who has lost his legs; he will never grow new ones. Therefore, once an alcoholic, always an alcoholic. For an alcoholic to drink again means they will die. What they did not realize is I treated my recovery as I did my addictions, with 100% commitment and every piece of energy I had in me. I used a solid foundation of sobriety, a collaboration of what I learned through both 12 step recovery programs.

I met my wonderful husband while working on my second cruise ship contract. He respected me, and was very sensitive and caring. He had a great sense of humor and loved children.

We would talk about how we wanted lots of children – at least 10.

We dreamed about getting married one day and how we would love to take a cruise in Alaska again, but as passengers together. We did not know how many children God would bless us with, but we knew we wanted to adopt, also. He and I had always worked with children so we had a merciful heart for children without parents.

> *"Be glad for all God is planning for you. Be patient in trouble, and always be prayerful. When God's children are in need, be the one to help them out. And get into the habit of inviting guests home for dinner or, if they need lodging, for the night."* Romans 12:12-13 (NLT)

How have your loved ones supported you in the healthy choices you have made?

Everything in life, matters

After my cruise ship contract, I got off the ship but left something behind. It was not my luggage, but my heart. My future husband was still on the ship working for another two months. I prayed that our relationship would endure a long distance relationship when he returned to England.

I had to find a job quickly when I got home. I had worked as a case manager in a mental health agency for children. I had worked in alcohol and drug treatment facilities. But after applying for many jobs, I still was unemployed after two weeks of being home.

I applied at a hair salon as the receptionist. One lesson I learned at the salon is that I will always respect receptionists, fast food workers, secretaries or any other customer service positions. I was treated by the salon clientele as if I were the trash under their shoe. Little did they know, I had six years of college education, had traveled the world and had gained more respect for myself than many of them will ever experience for themselves.

Becoming aware of my value in this life, I started working out and quit smoking. It had been my 700th attempt – at least it felt that way – to quit, but this time it was different. I used the 12 steps and realized how powerful nicotine's addiction was over me.

Be careful what you pray for, I had prayed a week before, *Please God take away my addiction to nicotine.* God did for me what I could not do for myself. Every puff off those next few cigarettes gave me a headache. My jaw locked up and I felt sick to my stomach. I still remember the day I was driving down the road, smoking a menthol cigarette I had bummed off someone. I took one puff off that cancer stick, looked at it and said Goodbye by throwing it out the car window. As soon as I did that, I felt fear engulf my whole being! What have I done? How will I live life without smoking? What will I do when I feel angry or stressed?

In July 2012, I celebrated 11 years smoke-free. God will deliver you of your addictions if you place them in His hands.

> *"I command you-be strong and courageous! Do not be afraid or discouraged. For the Lord your God is with you wherever you go."* Joshua 1:9 (NLT)

What brings you fear in your life? How can you lean on God to feel faith instead of fear?

The roof did not cave in!

*T*hroughout my sobriety, I started attending spiritual services, but not church. God forbid if I ever went into a church for more than a wedding. I truly thought that the roof would cave in and God would strike me dead with lighting if I walked into a church.

In the rooms of the program, I met the most remarkable, strong women. Women who if we had known each other when we drank, we would probably have all fought one another. In recovery program I was told, *"The men will slap your bum but the women will save it!"* There is a lot of truth to this saying. At the darkest times of my sobriety, these women were there for me when I had to call for help at 2 a.m. They were there celebrating a sober birthday, inviting me to a sober New Year's Eve party, and making sure I felt comfortable in my own skin.

I had two sober female friends who were so much fun to be around. We would laugh and laugh every time we hung out. They started attending this church in my hometown. The one says to me, *"If I can walk in there and worship, you could definitely go in there and the roof would not cave in on you!"* Till this day, I laugh at that, but it was so true. I thought there was no way with all the sins I committed that God would ever forgive me. We started attending every Sunday and it saved my life. No, really, Jesus saved me.

> *"The Lord is a shelter for the oppressed, a refuge in times of trouble. Those who know your name trust in you, for you, O Lord, have never abandoned anyone who searches for you."*
> Psalm 9: 9-10 (NLT)

Do you understand how precious you are to God? How do you know this?

You are forgiven!

I joined a membership class at the church I attended. I remember a picture being shown to me of Jesus standing at a door. It was a nice picture but the one detail I noticed right away was that the door did not have a door knob on the side where Jesus was standing. But it did have a door knob on the other side where the person was standing and opening the door towards them. The teacher of the class explained that Jesus is always there for us, we just have to open the door to Him. That hit home for me. I had made God and Jesus irrelevant for many years of my life. I never opened the door; in fact, I slammed the door on them numerous times.

In that class, I was also taught that when we accept Jesus as our Savior and admit our sins, God does not write them on a chalk board and just erase them. He destroys that chalk board. Jesus paid the ultimate price for my sins. I will never know how much it cost to see my sin upon that cross.

Later, I was submerged in baptism, and this time I got my hair wet and it did not concern me that I looked a mess afterwards. I felt beautiful, clean, and as white as the morning snow.

> *"For God so loved the world that he gave his only Son, so that everyone who believes in him will not perish but have eternal life. God did not send his Son into the world to condemn it, but to save it."*
> John 3:16-17 (NLT)

Have you forgiven yourself of all your sins? Is your lack of forgiving yourself holding you back from believing in Jesus?

Jesus Freak

Today, I am a Jesus Freak. I truly opened my heart and the depth of my soul to God's son, Jesus, who was born a man, lived a sinless life, healed the sick, used the poor and lost to save thousands, was crucified and rose from the dead for my sins. Today, my life is not about me and what I can get out of it. It is about whom I can help. And what I can give.

Why do some people not believe in Jesus Christ? I can only speak of me and my lost ways in the past. I never imagined in a million years the love, faithfulness, forgiveness and trust that God shows me every day through His son, Jesus.

As an early believer, I had to read children's Bible stories to understand what Jesus did for me. The stories are not of those that were born perfect and had no sin. He transformed the lives of the hopeless, the rotten, and the scum of the earth (as some people would call them).

Today, I do not challenge the Bible. I do not challenge other religious beliefs or non-believers. I try to do my best, and sometimes not very well at all, to live my life as Jesus did.

He loved everyone and wanted to show them the Light of the Life.

> *"What is faith? It is the confident assurance that what we hope for is going to happen. It is the evidence of things we cannot yet see."* Hebrews 11:1 (NLT)

When someone looks at you, do they see the light of Jesus? How do they see that? Are you forgiving to others?

Just keep loving him

My husband and I married in early 2003 and were immediately ready to start building our family. He was 31 years old and I was 28. When I met my husband in 2001, he was a Jew turned atheist. I remember praying to God that I wanted a good, Christian man. God would repeatedly tell me, *"Tina, just keep loving him."*

When my husband moved from England to Ohio to marry me, I would attend church two times a week; once on a Sunday for church service, and once during the week for a 12-step Bible Study. I invited my husband-to-be every time.

He did have to attend church for pre-marital counseling with me. My husband-to-be met our awesome, down to earth Pastor (who would marry us) and introduced himself as "I'm Warren, I'm a Jewish atheist. I don't believe in God, so I don't wanna hear it!"

Our Pastor responded back with "I'm Pastor Roger, the head pastor at this church and in our church we praise Jesus. Keep coming back!"

Within two weeks, he attended one church service. He enjoyed it. It was very different from the Synagogue he grew up in as a Jew in England. There were electric guitars, drums and a beat he could not resist tapping his foot to.

My husband loves to sing and had been a performer his whole life. So, after less than two months of attending church, he received Jesus into his heart through baptism, was singing on the Praise Team and assisting youth in drama skits. And to think, way back when we met God kept telling me, *"Just keep loving him."* Thank God, He loved us so much He saved us.

> *"They replied, Believe on the Lord Jesus and you will be saved, along with your entire household."* Acts 16:31(NLT)

Do you understand how much God loves you? How has He shown you?

How's your brother?

I was working at a great place teaching adults and children in alcohol and drug treatment. I loved this job! I loved the people, my co-workers and the duties. It was at this place of employment, I met my bestie, Margaret.

One morning, the adult students were walking into one of my educational classes and I recognized one young man.

Remember the earlier story about the last time I drank for 13 hours straight? The young man who walked into my class that day was the brother of the friend I drank with that long day and night. His brother was the one who, after 13 hours of drinking and all the alcohol had run out, I yelled at because how could he allow all the alcohol to be gone?

I was so excited to see his brother that I gave him a huge hug and asked, *"How's your brother?"* I was stunned when the young man looked down sadly and said, *"He's dead."*

"He's dead?" I questioned. *"What do you mean 'He's dead?'"* The young man fought back tears and answered, *"He died."*

His brother was 26 years old when he died. He was one of my friends in college for four years. I remember he was always there for me to make me feel better. And I also remember having lunch with him when I got sober and I shared with him my new found freedom and faith. I truly believe if I had continued drinking with him, I, too, would have died.

> *"My wound is desperate, and my grief is great. My sickness is incurable, but I must bear it."*
> Jeremiah 10:19 (NLT)

How has the death of a loved one changed you and your life?

With God, it's 100%!

*A*fter a year of trying to conceive a child, our Family Doctor suggested we go to an Infertility Specialist. I had no clue who that would be and what they did, but I followed instruction to do so.

The office was extravagant; marble floors, tables and fancy waiting room chairs. It appeared to be a Greek Palace of conception! I felt confident we had chosen a very successful fertility doctor and could not wait to have our baby's picture on the wall or in the lovely photo album that sat on the table anxiously awaiting our newest addition's portrait.

Success stories scattered the waiting room filled with pregnant women, most of them pregnant with multiples. Some women sat with their young children while newly pregnant. Then there were other women I noticed who did not pick up the photo albums, the women who sat off in the corner of the waiting room, the women who had not conceived through the help of fertility treatments and may never conceive their own children.

The first visit was simple; blood work, overall physical, internal and external ultrasounds, dye being shot up in my fallopian tubes to make sure they were not blocked, etc. My husband was examined as well. After all the poking and prodding, the doctor received all the results and the time had come for the final diagnosis.

PCOS was my diagnosis, Polycystic Ovarian Syndrome. I had no clue what it meant or why after eight years of sobriety, eight years of full-time employment, finally meeting the man of my dreams and becoming a devoted Christian woman...why would I have to be diagnosed with this condition? The doctor explained I would have a 15% chance of becoming pregnant *with* fertility treatments. My husband and I were in shock, disheartened and feeling a bit faithless. We agreed to begin a regime of medications, shots and artificial insemination.

The medications caused me to feel moody, over sensitive, and highly irritable. I started gaining weight, and my mornings consisted of waking up before 7 a.m., traveling to the Fertility Treatment Center for blood work and an internal ultrasound every morning to see the progress of my developing eggs. Each time I walked into that waiting room, I sat in the corner... the worthless, not-a-real-woman corner. Or so I thought, that was what I had become. I felt like a broken woman. How could God allow me to mess up my body so bad? Why is this happening to me?

"And Jesus said, Come to me, all of you who are weary and carry heavy burdens, and I will give you rest. Take my yoke upon you. Let me teach you, because I am humble and gentle, and you will find rest for your souls. For my yoke fits perfectly, and the burden I give you is light. "
Matthew 11: 28 (NLT)

Do you understand that Jesus takes your burden off you? How has He carried you through your weariness?

How can this be?

*M*y emotions were as if I were on a merry-go-round and the conductor got drunk and sped it up a thousand times. One minute, I would allow myself to dream of the day I would give birth to my own child, and the next minute, I would feel as if God forgot about me. I felt sad, then excited; disappointed, then hopeful. I hope to never have to undergo such an emotional roller coaster ever again. This was a very traumatic time in my life. The bedside manner of my specialist did not help my fragile state of mind.

My doctor had mentioned at an earlier internal ultrasound that I had produced three 'juicy' eggs that he will fertilize with my husband's sperm. He made a comment about having triplets. My husband and I quickly ran out and bought a mini-van to occupy our new triplets that would be blessing us in nine months!

The moment finally came that we had anticipated. After a month of powerful medications, fertility specialist appointments and intense treatments, we were going to have artificial insemination. The insemination occurred, not an eventful moment for me at all.

After cramping and numerous other appointments to evaluate my hormone levels through more blood tests, the day arrived to find out if our little triplets were developing as planned. I will never forget that day: November 4, 2004.

My husband and I walked into the waiting room. I sat in the Hopeful Mother spot browsing through portraits and wondering what our three little babies would look like. What would we name them? How would we get their photos taken for the Ultimate Baby Maker Album in the middle of the waiting room?

Without skipping a beat, or patient (which was usually 100 women a day for this specialist), he called for my husband and I to enter his glorious baby making office! It was decorated as if a Greek Baby God occupied it full-time. He sat on his throne among a marble desk with fancy gold desk ware. He reviewed our paperwork and test results and suggested, Well, like I said to you before, you had a 15% chance with fertility treatments to conceive. And unfortunately, this is not the time. Let's triple your medications and try this again next month!

Quickly he scribbled his signature on the prescriptions for more medications and acted as if we were just denied for a credit card. I could not help but think, this man is getting paid no matter what, and here we are, forking out over $8,000, and what do we go home with? Nothing. Depressed, heartbroken and feeling less of a woman than before, I took the prescriptions, stood up and complied with his instructions. My numb body got up and left his office, my husband remained silent as we walked through that cold, hard, heartless waiting room to the elevators. We walked out to the mini-van that we hoped would occupy our triplets one day. We cried together, we felt angry together and we stayed together.

Before the disastrous journey of fertility treatments, my husband and I discussed how maybe it is God's will for us to adopt children. We began praying about it and felt this was definitely what God wanted us to do. We began adoption parenting trainings, 30 hours in total, along with the completion of a home study which consisted of at least three home visits of a social worker that asked an array of questions about our family, friends, jobs and emotional well being. We felt hopeful again that maybe one day, we will have a baby to occupy our newly decorated nursery.

During this whole time, I worked at an Alcohol and Drug Treatment Center for adolescents. I was facilitating a group one night which included a 14 year old girl who was eight months pregnant and had tested positive for a drug. I remember feeling a moment of resentment, anger and disgust.

I could not help but think, that young lady could be carrying our baby. I felt a sense of mercy and empathy for her. I decided at that moment, God has a purpose for every life and every person. I was confident God wanted us to adopt a child to complete our family.

After many months of focusing on adoption, yet continuing one fertility medication to help me ovulate, I never imagined I would be blessed with becoming pregnant. I was 30 years old and now I was diagnosed with a tumor. An MRI indicated it was a solid mass and connected to all my nerves and muscle in my arm. The doctor predicted a five hour surgery and more than likely a cancerous outcome. We immediately turned to our church family. I was anointed at church for the tumor to be healed and that I would become pregnant.

Our baby was conceived with God's holy hand orchestrating it all. The Holy Spirit healed my once solid, more than likely cancerous tumor and blessed us with a baby. You see, after the tumor was removed, I had some pain in my pelvic area. My husband said, *"We are going to the ER!"* We rushed there and within 30 minutes were told we were pregnant, the baby was in my tube, my tube had ruptured causing internal bleeding and I had to have emergency surgery to remove my tube and living baby, the child we waited three years for, the baby we were told only had a 15% chance of being conceived through fertility treatments, the baby

God blessed us with. We chose to have the baby and tube removed in the morning. I was released from the Labor and Delivery Room and sent home before the major surgery in the morning.

> *"Children are a gift from the LORD; they are a reward from him."* Psalm 127:3 (NLT)

During a trial in your life, how has God brought you through it?

Hope for a good future

I remember that night, I lay awake crying, Why me? Why is this happening to me? Why can't I just get pregnant and have a normal baby like a lot of other women? Then Jeremiah 29:11 rang throughout my ears: *"For I know the plans I have for you, says the Lord. They are plans for good and not for disaster, to give you a future and a hope."*

A peace overwhelmed me. God has a plan and it is an awesome plan! The next morning, I woke up patient, calm and hopeful in God's plan for us. I entered the surgery room with confidence God had His hand in all this and would guide the surgeon's hand. Then, the surgery was over; I was no longer having a baby growing in my tube. I was no longer pregnant... or so I thought.

After the surgery, my husband and I traveled to Florida for a 2-week vacation. This visit to see his parents had been planned for months. I felt broken but at the same time hopeful because if God blessed me with one pregnancy, He would most definitely bless me again with just one tube and PCOS.

Our Florida vacation was perfect. I was able to rest, recover and prayed every day. I found comfort in the Bible:

"LORD, you know the hopes of the helpless. Surely you will hear their cries and comfort them." Psalm 10:17 (NLT)

Have you felt God's comfort in a life changing situation? How did it feel?

I am what?

I felt human again, hopeful and most of all, special that God chose us to have an opportunity to become parents to our own birth child. At a follow up doctor's appointment, the doctor said he had to remove my ruptured tube and my living baby because there was so much internal bleeding I would have died.

I was confident in God's timing, God's will and God's miracle, that one day we would hold our own birth child. My church family was incredible; supportive, helpful and most of all, prayerful! The Worship Pastor posted a prayer on his door asking everyone to pray every time they entered his office. People signed their signatures to that prayer and we have it framed hanging on our wall.

In June, my family was over for dinner. My sister mentioned I should take a pregnancy test. Mind you, I had taken over 20 pregnancy tests in the last three years. I swear, every time I had gas I would take a pregnancy test thinking maybe this time it was a baby moving! If my breasts felt sore, I would take a pregnancy test in hopes to see that line.

I entered the bathroom as if I was walking to the beat of a drum: boom, boom, boom, boom; the dreaded march to the doom of hopelessness, disappointment and despair to that bathroom to urinate on that life changing stick.

> *"When doubts filled my mind, your comfort gave me renewed hope and cheer."*
> Psalm 94:19 (NLT)

What hopes do you have today through the love of Jesus?

Praise Him in the storm

This time, it was different. I knew that no matter what, God had my back. God was in control, God had an awesome plan. I did my business, and with great surprise... the line shined like a huge, distinctive line of greatness. I was pregnant. I showed my sister and we shared it with my family. My husband, of course, felt skeptical. He said maybe it is just the hormones from being pregnant before, maybe it was from all the hormones from fertility treatments, maybe it was a mistake.

I said nothing in God's plan is a mistake! But, one thing was strange as my husband and I sat in the doctor's office listening to our baby's heartbeat, we realized we could not have conceived since surgery. This child had to be the twin of the baby removed from my ruptured tube.

Everything that a doctor warns a pregnant woman about happened during my pregnancy. I bled most of my pregnancy, I had cramps, I had a challenging time but I was pregnant and it was in God's timing. Nevertheless, I had that tumor removed from my arm and my tube with baby removed, and this unborn child survived all that.

In December, two months before my due date, I started labor. My doctor stopped it and I had to undergo steroid shots to develop the baby's lungs. I was put on bed rest and even though my husband and I kept telling the doctor there was no chance the baby was conceived after my surgery, he would not listen. Almost a month before my delivery date, I went into labor. This time our anxious trip to the hospital, the fourth time that week, we would be greeting our very own baby!

I will never forget that moment, after the third push, seeing my baby's face. He was angelic, precious and more than I could ever imagine. The nurses and doctor were expecting a premature baby, instead out came a 8 lb. 4 oz. healthy, big baby boy!

He was the surviving twin of the baby who was in my tube that ruptured and had to be removed. My husband held our new baby and said *I've waited my whole life for you.* This baby was named Victor because through it all he was victorious! He was named after my husband's grandfather.

I will never forget that moment of realizing how special my husband was. Here is a man that was the only male born to a Jewish father in Europe. His mother and father think very highly of their son and vice versa. The only wish my husband had his whole life was to have his own birth son to pass on the family name.

Even through this journey that God orchestrated perfectly for us, my husband never moaned or groaned that I could not produce a child, much less a son for him. This man was dragged to marriage counseling before we were married and for many years afterwards. He always loved me, supported me and most of all accepted responsibility. I will respect and love my husband all my life because of his demonstration of how a real Godly man should love and respect his wife no matter what she can offer him.

So, here we are with our precious son, both working in our careers, happy as can be. I continued to take care of myself physically, emotionally, spiritually and psychologically. We were blessed with traveling to England and Greece when our son was just one and a half years old. He got to meet his family in England and we had a lovely celebration of his sister's wedding in Greece. Life was fulfilling and exciting.

> *"The faithful love of the LORD never ends! His mercies never cease. Great is his faithfulness; his mercies begin afresh each morning. I say to*

myself, The LORD is my inheritance; therefore, I will hope in him!" Lamentations 3:22-24 (NLT)

Looking back on your life, can you see how God orchestrated your life? Explain how…

Enjoy where you are on the way to where you're going

*I*n June 2008, I felt called to stay home with my son. I resigned from my full-time job and ran a business out of my home. It was a dream come true opportunity. I worked when I wanted and played with my son when I wanted. It was incredible.

On a beautiful warm summer day, it shattered. I left my socks on after going for a run and went to walk down the painted, cement steps in the garage and slipped. As I fell down, I remember the hard, cold cement step pushing through my back as I violently fell upon it. The force of the impact flipped my body toward a wood exterior door and the pressure of my body flung open the door. I landed with my face next to the dog cage and laying there thinking this was not going to be a good outcome. I was rushed to the ER by an ambulance and after nine days of being bed ridden, I found out I had fractured two transverse processes. I was bed bound for weeks.

My son would come to my side and ask, *Don't you love me anymore mommy?* I felt helpless, hopeless and powerless I could not take care of myself, let alone my son. Once again my family, church family and friends supported us and assisted me in daily activities. I felt blessed once again that God's grace and mercy restored my physical well-being.

> *"My heart is confident in you, O God; no wonder I can sing your praises! Wake up, my soul!"*
> Psalm 108:1 (NLT)

Try to thank Him before you ask please for something. Have you praised God today?

We are blessed with less

We traveled to Florida each year to visit my in-laws. We loved the beach, ocean, blue skies and continuous sunshine. I applied for jobs every time we visited.

On the way home in 2008, I asked my husband if he would ever consider moving to Florida. He said absolutely not, three reasons: my job, our house and our dog! I suggested we pray about it and God will reveal His will for us. Within 2 weeks of my husband's statement, he lost his job, we had to foreclose on our house due to not being able to pay our mortgage on one income and our dog died. Soon after all that, God blessed me with a career opportunity in Florida. If your heart is open and your mind's not narrow, God will reveal His plan. It is a matter of having your eyes open to see it.

Since moving to Florida, we have grown spiritually by leaps and bounds. My husband was unemployed for at least six months when we first moved to Florida. We struggled with a limited income and no financial assistance. We are so grateful we found a church that supported us through a rent payment assistance program one month and the food pantry. God continued to bless us. I had numerous jobs, not by my decision but because God is so good He placed me where He wanted me to be. I met some of the strongest Christian women during these next few years.

Our son was having difficulty with the separation from family and friends. I remember one day him asking *When will this vacation end so we can go back home?* It was cute but interesting that he considered Ohio to be his home.

> *"So I pray that God, who gives you hope, will keep you happy and full of peace as you believe in HIM. May you overflow with hope through the power of the Holy Spirit."* Romans 15:13 (NLT)

Do you trust that God will provide all your needs? What footwork do you need to do so that God will provide?

When we put our cares in His hands, He puts His peace in our hearts

*W*e felt called to another church closer to home, so we attended it and fell in love with it. The people were warm, supportive and my husband and I quickly became volunteers. During this time, we had our own business. I lost a wonderful job and we became Licensed Therapeutic Foster Parents.

You see, God blessed us with one birth child but that blessing does not mean other children got the family they wanted, too. There were still many children out there parentless and hopeless.

God blessed us with a 15 year old foster son, a child that had lost all hope and faith in God. We demonstrated Jesus' love for him by bringing him into our home and hearts. Our son had a 'big bruder' he never would have had.

We were proud of this young man and watched as he went from stealing items to fulfill his basic needs to being a strong, confident student and athlete. After 1½ years, this young man chose to move out to live with another family. We were heartbroken but also realized it was all in God's plan. There was a reason for that season.

We still pray and love this child. We pray his life is full of success, peace and relationships built on unconditional love. He will always be welcomed in our home because he is already in our hearts.

> *"This I declare of the Lord: He alone is my refuge, my place of safety; he is my God, and I trust him."* Psalm 91: 2 (NLT)

How has God created you to reach out to orphaned children? Are you being called to work with these loving children? Become a foster/adoptive parent?

My brain just can't stop!

Our son continued doing exceptionally well academically at school but struggled with his behavior. It seems he inherited his mother's sense of curiosity and living a fast paced life. With so much to do and see, his impulsivity hurried him through each day to fulfill his need to accomplish his goal: to accomplish as much as he can in less time than anyone else!

After months of trying every behavioral modification program, dietary changes, an evaluation by a psychologist and primary care physician, we resorted to medication to help him neurologically with his impulsivity and ability to focus more. We feel this decision has secured his safety. He now feels confident about his everyday actions instead of being sad, depressed and disappointed in himself for his behavior.

We are praying that one day he will not need to be on medication for his hyperactivity. Research shows that his forever developing brain will benefit from it now and will be jump started, so that in the future, longevity use will not be necessary. We are prayerful he will be healed and given the focus he needs to maintain a productive life inside and outside the classroom.

> *"For all who are led by the Spirit of God of God are children."*
> Romans 8:14 (NLT)

How has a diagnosis helped you recognize your need for help from a doctor?

I pray 3 times a day

I pray once in the morning, once at night, and all day. I have learned not to worry about anything; instead pray about everything. And to think, at one time before I believed in God, I thought that God did not have time for me and surely did not want to hear my prayers. There were people dying who are devoted Christians and great people who needed God to hear their prayers, not mine. I thought to myself, I am not special enough to have God care for me or even love me.

God not only cares about me, but He gave His only begotten son to prove that He loves me, forgives me and cares about me. Even when I am asleep, He is cutting a deal for me.

> *"What can we say about such wonderful things as these? If God is for us, who can ever be against us?"* Romans 8:31 (NLT)

How have your negative thoughts caused you fear of living a faithful life?

God will always bring light to your darkness

While attending school and with his behavior improving, my son endured one of the worst nightmares a parent could imagine. The first time we allowed our child to visit a neighbor's house alone, he was abused by three older children. I was crushed and saddened that God would allow this to happen, but most of all my heart broke because my child no longer had that light for the Lord. My biggest nightmare was coming true. I prayed many nights that my son would live in light and be the light to others so they could see Jesus.

Our son became anxious, nervous to go outside, sad, depressed and would say things like, *"I wanna' cut my head off, I'm just so stupid!"* It broke our hearts and I called upon my prayer warrior friends. Each of them had prayer with me on the phone and promised to pray every day for our son.

All my years of working in social services kicked in, I called the necessary support services to get help for my son immediately. Within two weeks, he was attending intense therapy. One morning he cried before I dropped him off at school. He asked *Why did you let me get hurt at that house Mama?* I responded with an apology and promise I would never let anyone ever hurt him again. With the satisfaction of relief, he said okay Mama and left the car to go into school.

With many prayers protecting his spirit, he shared progress with me one morning. It was a rainy, stormy morning with gray clouds, a misty rain and a chill in the Florida air. Not a piece of blue sky or bright cloud in sight; it was a miserable day. Our son looked up and over to the east. There was one bit of light coming through the cloudy sky. It was one of those sights that looked as if God's light was traveling down from heaven on God's mission to save someone's spirit.

Our son found excitement at the sight and shouted, *"Look mama, there's God!"* At that moment, I knew God had healed his heart, lit his light even brighter than before and that our child was healed!

I am confident in knowing God has a purpose for our child and with that experience, he will help many others recover from their abuse.

I hear people ask all the time, *"If there was a God, why does He allow murder to happen?"* If you are one of those people, I want to ask you these questions: Who makes the sun rise and the sun set? Where is the sun when there's a tornado? Who is responsible for the miracles and joyous occasions in life?

I will tell you why God allows murder to happen – so that people like me will become committed Christians to save others through writing a book like this one. There are many miracles that are created out of disasters, horrific events and tragedies. The struggle is not why God allows it; the question should be, what will we do to help people understand that there is a God, and that His will for us is not to defeat us?

> *"The Lord is my light and my salvation - so why should I be afraid? The Lord protects me from danger - so why should I tremble?"* Psalm 27: 1(NLT)

How has the devil tried to defeat you?

Being uncomfortable is okay

*L*ying in the sand with the bumps that seashells make under your resting body can make for a stressful, uncomfortable situation. You just want to jump up and rake the sand to make it smooth beneath you so you can melt into the warm, soft sunlight.

To be uncomfortable can be miserable for some people. They have no control, they cannot predict their future outcomes, they do not believe in a Higher Power to provide their basic needs. God allows us to become uncomfortable because it is God making us change. My favorite saying is if it doesn't challenge you, it doesn't change you!

As human beings, we often get complacent in our everyday routines. We may have to move out of that uncomfortable spot to smooth out that part of the sand. Maybe use a tool to make our life easier, or maybe call upon Jesus to heal our broken hearts.

Some people think, if we live in a life of denial, telling ourselves the hurt is not that bad, then the uncomfortable feeling will go away. And then we remain complacent, resisting change.

But, in fact, God just gave us an opportunity to grow in our faith and we did not trust in Him.

> *"Trust in the Lord and do good. Then you will live safely in the land and prosper. Take delight in the Lord, and he will give you your heart's desires."* Psalm 37: 3-4 (NLT)

What uncomfortable situation have you been in lately? What was God teaching you?

Keep it simple

Often we listen for God to speak to us. We talk and cry, talk and cry to Him. We ask, *"Why me?"* But, do you ever give Him time to speak to you? We are busy; we work, we shop, we organize, clean and take care of others. But who takes care of you?

God does. So, instead of playing that computer game, texting your favorite friend on your phone or being impatient at the red light, take those moments to listen to God. Keep it simple by having the faith that God will see you through whatever He brings you to. Be quiet, be still and listen. God listens to you all the time; just be quiet and listen to Him for once.

> *"The Lord is close to all*
> *who call on him, yes, to all*
> *who call on him sincerely."*
> Psalm 145: 18 (NLT)

When will I take a moment to listen to God today?

But Mommy, other kids make fun of me

*A*s Christians, scripture tells us, *"Yes, and everyone who wants to live a godly life in Christ Jesus will suffer persecution."* 2 Timothy 2:12. Christians are covered by the armor of God, strong on the outside only because of God's grace; soft on the inside because of God's mercy.

My son always says when I say to him God made you very special. *"But Mama, other kids make fun of me."* I tell him that it does not matter what others think, the only person you have to make happy is God.

My son knows God loves him, God is trustworthy and God is always there for him. Our son has the spiritual gift of mercy, like my husband and I. He loves helping people. When others cry; he cries. He is very empathic and sympathetic. When we moved to Florida, my son was three years old, and he insisted we carry fruit and water in the car to hand out to homeless people on the corner.

One day, my son came home from school and said, *"Mama, I did what you told me!"* This statement kind of scared me to be honest. Curious, I asked him what he had done. He said, *"That bully came up to me at recess and yelled at me and just before he hit me, I asked him something!"* Scared to death, I asked what he asked him. My son said, *"I asked him, 'How can I pray for you, because you seem pretty miserable!'"*

I taught my son to pray for everyone, especially those who make fun of us or hurt us.

> ***"The Lord himself watches over you! The Lord stands beside you as your protective shade."***
> Psalm 121: 5 (NLT)

How can you pray for someone who has angered you? Would you be willing to ask someone today how you can pray for them?

Praise Jesus

*S*ince my child has been young, people would say how cute he is; what a charmer, a great talker and most of all, how funny he was. As his mother, I wish I could take all the credit, but I cannot. I am a sinner. I give all credit to Jesus. So when someone would say *you're so cute* to my son, I taught my son to say, *"Praise Jesus!"*

> *"For we are God's masterpiece. He has created us anew in Christ Jesus, so that we can do the good things he planned for us long ago."* Ephesians 2:10 (NLT)

Does your ego and pride stand in the way of seeing who really deserves the credit?

Looking for that perfect seashell

*H*ow many times have you been walking at the beach looking for that perfect seashell? Living so close to the beach, I try to go at least once a month and either lay on the beach to relax or walk the beach for exercise. Whatever your motive, the next time you are on the beach, I want you to find the most disgusting, beat up, ugly shell. You may need to clean it up because it may have sea slime on it. Maybe a bird defecated on it. Maybe there are holes in it. Hold on to that shell and pray over that shell. Keep it close to you.

We as humans walk the beach and look for the most perfect, beautiful shells while leaving other shells behind. We pass up some beautiful shells, maybe a Star fish without one of its arms, or a broken sand dollar.

I thank God every day that He did not pass me up while I lay waiting for Him to pick me up. You see, when I did not believe in God, I felt disgusting, beat up, ugly and rejected, hurt and most of all, worthless.

> *"There are three things that will endure-faith, hope, and love-*

and the greatest of these is love." 1 Corinthians 13: 13 (NLT)

Today, I am grateful God chose me, loved me and kept me. Are you that perfect seashell or did God have to brush you off and make you beautiful and whole again?

Can you hear the waves?

When was the last time you heard birds chirp and sing? When was the last time you listened to what your child is really saying to you? When was the last time you listened to the wave's crash against the seashore? If you are still thinking… maybe it's time to slow down. Be still in God's presence. Listen to His guidance. Stop and just be.

> *"And so, dear brothers and sisters, I plead with you to give your bodies to God because of all he has done for you. Let them be a living and holy sacrifice - the kind he will find acceptable."* Romans 12:1 (NLT)

How can you be at peace today?

How to take control when you admit you're powerless

I believe people run from reality for four reasons:

1. Fear of the unknown,
2. Fear of the known,
3. Fear of change, and lastly
4. Fear of the truth.

Let's start with the first one: fear of the unknown. I think people use alcohol, drugs and other addictions to run from the unknown. We live in a society that is quick to say it's better when it's cheap, fast and easy! Remember, it's okay to feel uncomfortable.

Real life and worthwhile things are the opposite. Have you ever heard the saying *Everything good in life is worth the wait?* It's true. Nothing really worth having will come easy, cheap, or fast!

Another reason people use addictions to escape reality is the fear of the known. What do you know? Usually, what you know is what you have experienced and you have your own feelings about that. But what if I was to tell you that those feelings are not facts? It's like this: when you question siblings in a family what was it like growing up, you will have multiple answers. Your experiences are what are known. But are they the truth?

The third reason why people escape through addictions is their fear of change. Let's face it; as human beings people do not like to change. Especially if they have thought, acted and felt the same way for 50 years. It gives a false confidence of control thinking you can predict the future all the time by not changing.

Remember, this is a society of easy, cheap and fast...now, you're saying, "*I have to acknowledge what is wrong and I have to actually change it?*" People have a difficult time accepting responsibility, being accountable, letting go and taking that action to change.

The last, but not least, reason people run is the fear of truth. Just maybe, you're not right all the time! Oh dear, this will hit some people right between the eyes. "*So, Tina, are you saying that maybe God is right and my opinion does not matter?*"

I will never forget when I first got sober. I had 30 days of sobriety. I was being mentored by a 82 year old man who had 45 years of sobriety. God bless him, that man lived, breathed, ate and dreamt this 12 step recovery program. He committed his whole life to the program and helping others.

One day, a woman was talking about her alcoholism and I opened my big, egocentric mouth. Mind you, I was 23 years old, had 30 days sober and thought I had it all figured out. That man was quick to tell me to, *"Shut up, you don't know anything about sobriety!"*

Wow, he was lucky I was not drinking at the time. When I was drinking and someone spoke to me like that, I would do one of two things: hit them or scream at them! But the one thing I learned in recovery was this: I was powerless, my life was unmanageable, I believed in God and trusted that He would restore me. I had tasted that humility early in sobriety. And I had also learned that if my first reaction to someone else is anger, I need to look at myself because they are probably telling the truth.

There's a rap song, Check yourself before you wreck yourself! I love it because it's so true. We have to ask ourselves why we are so affected by someone's words. Most of the time it is because it is the truth and we do not like to hear the truth.

> *"And the prayer offered in faith will make the sick person well; the Lord will raise him up. If he*

has sinned he will be forgiven."
James 5:15 (NLT)

What truth is quick to anger you? Are you willing to look at this issue and try to get help for it?

Do everything for God

*J*ust because I am writing this book, does not mean I am perfect. It does not mean I am the honorary recipient of Being The Perfect Christian award. I wake up some days and just want to do what I want to do. Sometimes on Sunday mornings, I want to sleep in, rest and have a lavish morning by myself.

I have realized that when I do not want to do something, then I do it for God. If I wake up and do not want to go to work, I do it for God. If I see someone I really do not fancy, I am kind to them for God. If I have a chore to do and really do not want to do it, I do it for God. As long as I do it for God, it takes me and my selfishness out of it and helps me live my life for God.

> *"Let all that I am praise the LORD; with my whole heart, I will praise his holy name."*
> Psalm 103:1 (NLT)

Who can you be kind to for God? What else can you do today for God?

Your children will become who you are; so be who you want them to be

I love this quote. When our son acts up and is disrespectful, I think of how I have been acting. It is hard sometimes to realize that how I have been acting has been selfish and not very thoughtful. Sometimes I am impatient with him and say things like, *"Hurry up, You are going to make me late to work!"* And sometimes what he hears me say is, *"You are not worth my time or energy and you are an inconvenience in my life!"*

I do not mean that and I do not want my child to ever think he is an inconvenience; after all, it was my physical actions with my husband and God's grace that created him. He was not asked to be born, or to be born to us as parents. How dare I project my lack of organization and time management on my child! Naughty me!

> *"Those who control their anger have great understanding; those with a hasty temper will*

make mistakes." Proverbs 14:26 (NLT)

How can you be an example of how Jesus wants you to live your life today? What have your loved ones seen in you that is not Christ like?

Inappropriate for children

*E*ver since our son was born, I never spoke baby talk. I have always explained things to him in great detail, using technical terms and then explaining what those mean as well.

This child was singing by the age of nine months old, and spoke paragraphs by the age of three. One of his first sentences to me when he was two years old was, *"Mama, we need to talk. About my life!"*

I was terrified when he said that. I remained calm and questioned if he was happy or not. He said yes, but he wanted to thank me for being his Mama and to find out what his purpose in life is. I was amazed at his vocabulary.

I only showed our son appropriate movies for his age while growing up. When he started watching TV cartoons I would say, *"That's not acceptable."* or *"That's inappropriate."*

One day, I was watching an adult movie. It was not X rated but there was some cursing in it. My son walked in covered his eyes and said, "*Oh Mama, that is inappropriate. Why are you watching that?"* It made me ponder this question: if you would not allow your child to see it or hear it why are you allowing yourself to do it?

> *"Don't use foul or abusive language. Let everything you say be good and helpful, so that your words will be an encouragement to those who hear them."* Ephesians 4:29 (NLT)

How can you control the trash you put into your head today?

The Power of Words

When you read:

"300,000 people die each day, enjoy your day!"

Does that motivate you? Now what if I were to say:

"Enjoy this beautiful God given day! 300,000 people will not!"

The Power of Words is amazing. Our words can break us down, or build us up.

> *"The tongue can bring death or life; those who love to talk will reap the consequences."*
> Proverbs 18:21 (NLT)

Will you help build someone up today by using encouraging words? Or will you break them down by using hurtful, painful words? The choice is yours. Or should I say, the power is yours?

Be brave and chill out

*M*y six year old son and I went to the dentist office. The dental hygienist came to the waiting room, called out my son's name and asked him to follow her. I lifted myself off the chair to follow them and she said, *"Oh no, just him. We'll be back for you in a little bit."* I felt fear, anxiety, and thought, *Slow down, Tina, and focus.* I listened for my son to cry, yell, or feel the same fear I felt while waiting so far away from him.

Instead, I heard him chatting to the x-ray technician, then to the dentist. He spent one hour back there, getting a dental cleaning by himself. When he was done, he came back to me while I sat in the chair to be seen by the dentist.

My son took my hand and said, *"Be brave, Mama, and chill out. It's not going to last forever!"* What great advice from a six year old. And everyone's fear is different; some people yell, some people get quiet and some people just get rude.

Next time when you are faced with a new situation, try to be brave, chill out and remember it's not going to last forever!

> *"This is what the Sovereign LORD, the Holy One of Israel, says: 'Only in returning to me and resting in me will you be saved. In quietness and confidence is your strength. But you would have none of it.'"*
> Isaiah 30:15 (NLT)

How often are you faced with an unfamiliar, unpredictable, or uncomfortable situation and freak out? How can you chill out and be brave?

Blessed for what I don't have

I do not have a brand name purse; I do not wear brand name clothing or drive a fancy car. If you do, that's great for you. I am just not into that sort of thing. I would rather spend extra money on a massage, pedicure or helping someone else out. But that's me. I am not saying I am special or that I am better. I am just making an observation.

I decided to go out on Black Friday for the first time ever in my life. I took my son because we went to the early bird specials before 9 p.m. I lasted 30 minutes. I have never experienced so many negative, rude, greedy people before in such a short amount of time. People were lined up for the latest video gaming system, the biggest TV, the most expensive jewelry and the newest big hit toy!

As eager and excited as these people were to get a deal, I could not help but think, *Will they be this eager to get into heaven?* And if they were, would they be this rude, greedy and negative?

My son and I left the store with a $6 pair of slippers and a $36 vacuum cleaner. Nothing in my life is worth the disrespect and drama of being that selfish and greedy. Today, I am blessed for what I do not have. And today, I am blessed because my life is not perfect, but God is.

> *"Don't weary yourself trying to get rich. Why waste your time? For riches can disappear as though they had the wings of a bird!"* Proverbs 23: 4-5 (NLT)

What are you grateful for that you do not have today?

Evil thoughts

A friend shared with me, *"Let evil thoughts be still born; do not birth them and give them life."* Evil thoughts will have evil consequences. This is true.

If I think it and say it, unfortunately, someone will feel it. Today, I will think before I speak and ask myself, is it:

        T   Thoughtful

        H   Honest

        I   Intelligent

        N   Necessary

        K   Kind

If it's all these, then I can say it.

When we call ourselves losers, ugly or unloving, what we are really doing is telling God His handiwork is not good enough. Would you criticize His handiwork in a beautiful sunset? Then stop disrespecting His master piece which is you.

"Wherever your treasure is, there your heart and thoughts will also be." Matthew 6: 21 (NLT)

What evil thoughts do you tell yourself? How can you change the way you treat yourself?

What's your motivation?

*A*sk yourself: *What is your motivation,* before it comes out of your mouth. If your motivation is to encourage someone, then say it. If it is to change or gain power over someone, then do not say it. If everyone would ask themselves what their motivation is before speaking all the time, we would have a much more peaceful world.

A transformation starts with the communication in your head, followed by the solution made by your heart. Quit talking about the changes you are going to make and start completing the actions that will transform you today!

> *"Teach us to make the most of your time, so that we may grow in wisdom."* Psalm 90: 12 (NLT)

How have you tried to control others through your words?

Don't talk yourself out of what God wants you to do

The day was coming for two months, my husband's last day of his full-time job. We had been sending resumes out for two months. We sent out over 86 resumes, all over the United States. God says, *"In due season, you will win!"*

The last time my husband lost his job, it was in 2009. It was one of the last resorts for us that initiated a move to another state to seek employment. This time it is different.

Up until 2009, we had stuff. We owned a house bigger than needed for the three of us, had a Jacuzzi, two cars, almost one acre of land, a big playground built for our son in the backyard and enough furniture packed in our house for five families. But, with all that stuff, came bills; credit card bills, loans, mortgages – lots of bills each month.

We thought we had it all figured. We would work in our full-time jobs till retirement. But God had another plan. When we moved to Florida to pursue a new life, new careers, and God's life for us, we had all our belongings in one moving truck. We had to file bankruptcy and foreclose on our house. Our one vehicle was repossessed. We had to sell all that new furniture, that Jacuzzi, and all we could take was our clothes, and most importantly, ourselves.

Would we have ever predicted that in just six years of marriage we would have to lose everything to gain it all? God stripped us of all the material things we had known and we had to rely on Him.

I remember the humility of asking the church to help with our rent; they so willingly assisted us with rent one month. I remember praying to God that we could afford milk, bread and eggs this month. The church and people at the church made sure our cabinets were filled each day. Our church family in Ohio sent us a fruit basket one day and it fed us for a week! No matter what you do not have, God has it and in abundance!

> *"Endure suffering along with me, as a good soldier of Christ Jesus. And as Christ's soldier, do not let yourself become tied up in the affairs of this life, for then you cannot satisfy the one who has enlisted you in his army. Follow the Lord's rules*

for doing his work, just as an athlete either follows the rules or is disqualified and wins no prize." 2 Timothy 2:3-5 (NLT)

Are you ready to receive God's abundance today? What fears of your future do you need to Let Go and Let God?

I balanced the checkbook and we have more than we started with!

I was called to work in social services with children in foster care. This was a population I had little experience with, so I was looking forward to it. I worked the hardest I ever have in a job during those six months. I got promoted and went from making $40K a year to $53K a year. That's like a millionaire pay in the child welfare field! I even began to mentor one of the young people in foster care. Unbeknownst to me, my Acting Supervisor had other plans.

I entered work, sat at my desk and worked non-stop managing a team of unbelievable case workers. I managed Federal and State grants. I called upon the community to help these children in foster care. Finally, I found a job that God created for me to succeed at and flourish to help others.

And then it happened, my Acting Supervisor walked into my office and asked me to join her in her office. I complied, as always, and followed her into her office. She screamed at me, and quickly followed up with, "*Since today is the last day of your probationary period, you have not successfully completed it."* The woman fired me because she felt I challenged her on mentoring a child when I asked if I could transport him to church with my family one Sunday.

I will never forget that moment. She fired me exactly four hours before my six month probationary period would be completed. She took away my income, my health insurance for my family and my dignity. In one sentence, her action cut like a sword through my heart and head.

Immediately, I called my husband, an attorney, and friends. Everyone was in shock! I was heartbroken, humiliated, and humbled but most of all, I felt sad that this child I was mentoring would miss out on experiencing church with my family.

God does for us what we cannot do for ourselves. Sometimes we do not understand what His plan is for us during the chaos but I called upon my prayer warriors; they prayed with me, cried with me and continued to be the hands of God.

I went from an income of $53K a year to $1000 a month with my unemployment income. That income did not even cover our rent for one month. Every time a bill was due, I would pray, *"Please God provide us with the means to pay this electric bill, water bill, or prescription."*

Every time I went to the mail box, there was a check. One time it was a check for over $700 for an insurance reimbursement, another time it was a check from an audit that was done at my back specialist's office in Ohio from 2008. Every day, God provided for us.

One day, I balanced my check book and realized, we ended the month with more money than expected. This money enabled us to drive over 20 miles each Sunday to pick up that foster child and bring him to church with us. It enabled us to fulfill God's will for our family and become Licensed Therapeutic Foster Parents to that young man. We were able to purchase a newer vehicle, move into a larger apartment to house this young man and feed all of us. You see, when we are in the mist of chaos, God had his paint brush creating the master piece. And His master piece is always that....a MASTER PIECE.

> *"So the Lord blessed Job in the second half of his life even more than in the beginning."* Job 42:12(NLT)

How will God bless you today? Remember, His will for us is always perfect and the best!

How can I pray for you?

The first time someone asked me this, I had a reaction many probably do. Why would you want to pray for me?

I remember when I did not believe in God and my life was a living hell because of it, I would think, *Don't other people have stuff to do in their lives other than pray for me? Why would someone take time to care about little ole' me? Why would anyone want to pray for me? Surely God has enough people to worry about besides me!*

Needless to say, I had no self-esteem, felt worthless and treated myself miserably. My mother used to send me cards in college in the mist of my addiction that read, *"Praying for you, Love you"*. During the depths of my darkness, I felt her prayers lift me out of the hole I had dug myself into.

Whenever anyone vents to me, moans and groans, I instantly ask them now, *"How can I pray for you?"* Because after all, isn't that what they are indirectly asking you to do? They need prayer, they want prayer, and their cry for pity is by griping about someone or something.

"Then he said, Don't be afraid, Daniel. Since the first day you began to pray for understanding and to humble yourself before your God, your request has been heard in heaven. I have come in answer to your prayer." Daniel 10:12 (NLT)

Today, ask someone that is getting on your last nerve, *"How can I pray for you?"* God will change your attitude and you may just be surprised at their explanation of how you can pray for them.

People Pleasers don't please the most important person

*I*t was always about everyone else. I wanted to make everyone happy, make life peaceful. I did not want to rock the boat. This is called being a People Pleaser. Today, I live my life to please God. The most important person to me is God, not me, not my loved ones and definitely not my child. The next time you think of pleasing someone and putting your needs aside, what will you do instead?

> *" And it is impossible to please God without faith. Anyone who wants to come to him must believe that God exists and that he rewards those who sincerely seek him."* Hebrews 11:6 (NLT)

Have you ever done something for someone and it was not good enough? Or they did not act the way you hoped they would react?

What if?

What if you were to choose to delete one day of your life? One day, maybe a day you were humiliated, a day you got fired, a day you found out your loved one died. Any one day, gone, never ever seen or heard about ever again. What day would it be and why?

> *"Those who are dominated by the sinful nature think about sinful things, but those who are controlled by the Holy Spirit think about things that please the Spirit. So letting your sinful nature control your mind leads to death. But letting the Spirit control your mind leads to life and peace."* Romans 8:5-6 (NLT)

How would it change your life? How would it change who you are today?

Is it your body or God's?

*S*o, you were born with a purpose and a healthy body? God's vision for your life has a lot to do with what we do to our bodies. How you treat your body now, will affect how your body will treat you in the future. Eat healthy, exercise, and stop putting all those bad chemicals in it. You only get one chance to treat yourself right.

For many years, I smoked cigarettes and marijuana, drank alcohol and was sexually active. I did not exercise or even cared if I ate a fruit or vegetable once a month, much less 4-5 fruits and vegetables a day!

In early 2007, after an office evaluation and blood work, I was diagnosed with Fibromyalgia and Rheumatoid Arthritis. It was that moment I had a choice: I could sit back, be a victim and have the *poor me's* or I could do everything possible to be healthy, exercise and take care of myself.

I chose the latter, I began running. My first goal was to run in a relay race. I would run 3.1 miles which I completed in September 2007. Even after a torn tendon in my knee, a broken back and the painful daily reminders of having arthritis, I still eat healthy and workout.

> *"Spend your time and energy in training yourself for spiritual fitness. Physical exercise has some value, but spiritual exercise is much more important for it promises a reward in both this life and the next. This is true and everyone should accept it."* 1Timothy 4:7-9 (NLT)

How will you respect God's temple, your body, today?

I am grateful today

Some days the Fibromyalgia and Rheumatoid Arthritis is non-existent; other days, the painful reminder creeps up on me when I am trying to sit on a toilet or walking upstairs. I try to never complain or pay much attention to my daily aches and pains.

As my foster son used to say, *There is a 4-year old child somewhere in a third world country making bricks!* In other words, I could have it a lot worse. Today, I exercise, eat healthy, get massages, do yoga, keep active and will not give into what I have been told by doctors.

> *"Or don't you know that your body is the temple of the Holy Spirit, who lives in you and was given to you by God? You do not belong to yourself, for God bought you with a high price. So you must honor God with your body."* 1 Corinthians 6:19-20

How does your daily lifestyle honor God?

Details, details...

One morning, I stood in a lobby, waiting for an elevator. I was trying to be patient, but the meeting I was attending was an important business meeting and it was located on the twenty sixth floor. So, I was not going to take the stairs in a suit with high heels. I waited and waited for the elevator, growing more and more restless. I started getting very angry pacing back and forth in front of the elevator, when I just happened to look down at the button on the wall and realized, I forgot to push it! So I pushed it and thought how that lesson can be a daily reminder to all of us.

How often do we go about our day and grow restless, impatient and angry?

> *"May God, who gives this patience and encouragement, help you live in complete harmony with each other, as is fitting for followers of Christ Jesus."* Romans 15:5 (NLT)

Have you prayed today?

The 3 A's

A problem identified is half solved. The first of the 3 A's is: Awareness, then Acceptance and Action. When you become aware of an issue you can then accept it or become angry about it. However, choosing anger will stop the process of growing. Accepting an issue or person will help you take the action to do what you need to do to make your life healthy and functional.

> *"Therefore, since we have been made right in God's sight by faith, we have peace with God because of what Jesus Christ our Lord has done for us."*
> Romans 5:1(NLT)

What can you pray about that you need help accepting? What action do you need to do to change that awareness?

The hardest part

I was working out 4-5 times a week before I injured my back again and had to stop. It was great and I loved meeting the people, a lot of inspiring people like this one older gentlemen in a wheel chair. He would get out of his car, struggle to walk to his trunk and get his wheel chair out and plop himself into it. He would use the joy stick to maneuver his automatic wheel chair into the workout facility. He would wheel himself into the pool area and swim for forty five minutes every day. The lady working at the desk said he's been swimming everyday for the last two years. What an inspiration to me! If this man can barely walk and still works out, what is my excuse?

As I was leaving, he was leaving the facility too. I opened and held the door for him to exit. I walked beside his speedy chair as we continued in the same direction toward our parked cars. I said to him, *Have a blessed day.* He said, *You, too.*

He then shouted to me as I was walking toward my car, *The hardest part of working out....is leaving!*

"The lazy person is full of excuses, saying, I can't go outside because there might be a lion on the road! Yes, I'm sure there's a lion out there!"
Proverbs 26:13 (NLT)

What excuses today have you used to not take care of yourself?

Jesus Saves!

One day on my way home from work, I noticed a man with a sign. He would hold up the sign and it read **Jesus Saves!** You could hear fellow Christians honking at him and waving. I would always honk the horn and wave at him. I looked forward to seeing him standing on the corner of the street every day. I would honk the horn and wave with excitement as if I saw a super star!

One day on my way home from work, I noticed that same man with a different sign. I could not read it too well, so as I got closer, I put my hand on the horn to honk in support. But as I got close enough to read the sign, it read **Judgment Day is Coming!**

I found myself not honking my horn, not smiling, not waving and not feeling very supportive. Please understand, I read the Bible, I understand Judgment Day but I have a negative reaction to Christians that shout that from the streets! As an atheist in the past, I was told numerous times that because I had sex before marriage (mind you, I was raped) that I was going to hell. I wanted to tell them, just because my sin looks different than yours, please don't judge me!

> *"For the LORD your God has arrived to live among you. He is a mighty savior. He will rejoice over you with great gladness. With his love, he will calm all your fears. He will exult over you by singing a happy song."*
> Zephaniah 3:17 (NLT)

Will you be the Christian holding the Jesus Saves sign today or the Judgment Day is Coming Christian?

There's more to me than what you see

In school, I loved meeting new people, visiting with friends but, most of all, feeling like the one that brings laughter and happiness to everyone. I was a silent sufferer for many years. In high school, I tried to treat everyone like the way I wanted to be treated. It did not matter which neighborhood you were from, who your parents were or what kind of grades you got or the sports you participated in; I judged you on how you treated me.

My senior year, I was crowned Homecoming Queen which surprised me because even though I enjoyed talking to everyone all the time, I felt like I was not a person that should be placed up on a pedestal, let alone on a throne with a crown. I would think, if only all these people really knew the real me, they would not be honoring me with a crown. I threw that crown in the bottom dresser drawer for years because I did not feel worthy enough for it.

" Therefore I, a prisoner for serving the Lord, beg you to

lead a life worthy of your calling, for you have been called by God. Always be humble and gentle. Be patient with each other, making allowance for each other's faults because of your love. Make every effort to keep yourselves united in the Spirit, binding yourselves together with peace."
Ephesians 4:1-3 (NLT)

Today, I know I am worthy because God loves me and all His children. However, I am not deserving of a crown because I am a sinner. Do you know you are worthy of God's love today?

Building walls

From a young age, I learned that if I built walls up around me, I was less likely to get hurt. So, I would form superficial relationships, share just enough with someone but not too much for fear of rejection. I thought these walls would protect me, but I realize now, that they only kept me from sharing my gifts with others.

Today, I will share my gifts with others, what they do with them is not my business. I will not live in fear everyday of being hurt but trust in the Lord. Everything happens for a reason and God has each person in my life for a season.

> *"There is a time for everything, a season for every activity under heaven. A time to be born and a time to die. A time to plant and a time to harvest."*
> Ecclesiastes 3: 1-2 (NLT)

How can you trust people enough to share the Word of Jesus with them?

The devil wants to define you by your bad choices. God wants to define you by your belief in His son.

I have worked with drug addicted people and criminals most of my professional life, over 15 years. What I find myself repeatedly saying on a daily basis is, you are not your crime or the choices you made! You are not defined by your bad choices. The devil is a liar! You can start your life over at any moment.

First become aware that you made bad choices. Second, accept that you have made these bad choices, don't make up excuses. Be accountable for your actions. I have also met many abused people who never turned to drugs or crime, so it's not an excuse to justify bad choices.

Furthermore, forgive yourself so you can start over. The number one trigger, I believe, that causes women to relapse with drugs is shame and guilt. Once you have forgiven yourself, you understand that you are not perfect and you will stop expecting others to be perfect.

When I got sober, the hardest thing for me to do was look into the mirror into my eyes and say *I forgive you.*

Forgiveness is a gift for you, not anyone else because they are not deserving of it. This is why you will no longer resent people. Remember, expectations are premeditated resentments. Accept people for who they are, sinners; they are not perfect. Progress rather than perfection!

> *"One day Jesus said to his disciples, There will always be temptations to sin, but what sorrow awaits the person who does the tempting!"* Luke 17:1(NLT)

How can forgiving yourself today help with your relationships with others?

You have a choice, search for solutions or seek forgiveness

When making Amends, be careful not to rip off scabs. Some people heal from the inside out through self-help support groups, therapy and forgiveness. Other people move on, and a thin scab covers the surface of the wound you caused. These wounds have not healed from within, and the hurt and pain are still there just under the surface.

You can make amends by changing you: your behavior, your attitude and your actions. A person would rather <u>see</u> a sermon any day then hear one.

> *"But I tell you, love your enemies! Pray for those who persecute you!"* Matthew 5: 44 (NLT)

How can you learn from God's word? How can you teach God's word? How can you be sure to put God first every day in your life?

Who's your Daddy?

I was a middle and high school teacher for a short time for female students. In that limited amount of time, God blessed me so much. All of my students were either in foster care and/or the juvenile justice system. Most of them were on probation for a crime they committed.

As you can imagine, my first day teaching them was challenging, especially since the circumstance was that their teacher unexpectedly had to be rushed to the hospital in labor. The girls were tough on me. Most of them did not want to give me a chance. I could not blame them; I had once felt like that, too.

God spoke to me that first day and said, *"The only difference between you and them, Tina, is that you have made it to the other side, full of love, forgiveness and joy."* I knew it was my mission to bring these gifts to them.

"You have a purpose! You are NOT a mistake!" As I spoke these words with passion, I started to see the tears in their eyes. *"I love YOU! Not for what you have done, not for who you are, but for what YOUR purpose is!"* In that statement, all the walls came down.

Some came up to me and hugged me. Some even shared with me that no one ever told them they were NOT a mistake. Some shared their drug addictions, severely abusive pasts and fears with me.

Another lesson I taught them is acceptance of a person as a valuable human being does not equate to accepting inappropriate actions. I taught them how to respect themselves and how to respect others.

One girl started to cry and said, "*Ms. Tina, I never met my father! If he cannot be there for me and love me, who can?*" I approached the crying, disheartened girl and began to tell her about who her real Daddy is! She was a believer and had already shared with me that she attends church and reads the Bible. A few other girls joined me; we placed our hands on her shoulders and began to pray. It was the most spiritual experience these young women might have ever had.

God brought me to that job for a purpose and it was to show these young women they have a purpose in life. I still keep in touch with some of them. The ones I do not communicate with, I still pray for and think of them often.

"The eyes of all look to you in hope; you give them their food as they need it. When you open your hand, you satisfy the hunger and thirst of every living thing." Psalm 145:15-16 (NLT)

Who is your Daddy today? Do you really understand how much He truly loves you?

Bridge to nowhere

*H*ave you ever felt like you were on a bridge to nowhere? Just traveling along, clueless as to what God has planned, but you do not have the feeling of jumping off that bridge – or maybe you do? As my family and I face a future of unforeseen circumstances with the recent lay off of my husband, I trust that God will provide for us. Now does this mean we sit back, kick up our feet and wait? No, after sending out over 86 resumes to job opportunities around the United States, we still have not heard from one as to even scheduling a phone interview. NOTHING!

How is it that my gifted husband, after 20 years of teaching and performing, cannot find a job? I am learning that not only do we trust in the Lord but we have to praise Him for this time. The time my husband has with our six year old son everyday over this Christmas break. The time my husband has to spend with his parents that are visiting from England. I am praising God that we are healthy and happy. Our financial freedom does not determine our future; our future will determine our freedom from the worries of finances.

I am trying to relax in His timing and His will for us. Faith is not believing that God can, it is knowing that God will.

> *"He asked you to preserve his life, and you granted his request. The days of his life stretch on forever. Your victory brings him great honor, and you have clothed him with splendor and majesty."* Psalm 20:4-5 (NLT)

How can you trust that God will take care of all your needs, including your finances today?

My gift to you

My prayer is that you have found some hope in my journey of lessons that became my blessings. My hope is that you will support my mission to help others through sharing my testimony and that you would pray for the salvation of so many others that are still struggling with self-sabotage and addictions.

I ask God to place His healing hand upon each of you, to heal your broken hearts by softening them and giving the gift of forgiveness to yourself and others.

Remember, while you're asleep, God is cutting a deal for you! In the quietness of His actions, we wait upon the Lord.

As a Christian, instead of judging others sins because they don't look like yours, ask them how you can pray for them.

May all your blessings continue to help you grow in the Lord and keep you focused on His will for you. Today, try to say thank you to God before asking please for anything else. Every day is a gift. Treat everyone as if today was your last day with them.

"I have much to tell you, but I don't want to do it in a letter. For I hope to see you soon, and then we walk face to face. May God's peace be with you. Your friends here send you their greetings. Please give my personal greetings to each of our friends there." 3 John 1:13-15 (NLT)

I pray you will join me in my future publications and speaking engagements.

Feel free to email me at tinamlevene@gmail.com or visit my websites:
www.tinamlevene.com &
www.truthfulmovementforfemales.com

 *Hopeful 4 u-Tina*